Contents

H CONTENTS

CONTENTS

Use of guidance

THE APPROVED DOCUMENTS

This document is one of a series that has been approved and issued by the Secretary of State for the purpose of providing practical guidance with respect to the requirements of Schedule 1 to and Regulation 7 of the Building Regulations 2010 (SI 2010/2214) for England and Wales.

At the back of this document is a list of all the documents that have been approved and issued by the Secretary of State for this purpose.

Approved Documents are intended to provide guidance for some of the more common building situations. However, there may well be alternative ways of achieving compliance with the requirements. **Thus there is no obligation to adopt any particular solution contained in an Approved Document if you prefer to meet the relevant requirement in some other way.**

Other requirements

The guidance contained in an Approved Document relates only to the particular requirements of the Regulations which the document addresses. The building work will also have to comply with the requirements of any other relevant paragraphs in Schedule 1 to the Regulations.

There are Approved Documents which give guidance on each of the Parts of Schedule 1 and on Regulation 7.

LIMITATION ON REQUIREMENTS

In accordance with Regulation 8, the requirements in Parts A to K and N (except for paragraphs H2 and J6) of Schedule 1 to the Building Regulations do not require anything to be done except for the purpose of securing reasonable standards of health and safety for persons in or about buildings (and any others who may be affected by buildings or matters connected with buildings).

Paragraphs H2 and J7 are excluded from Regulation 8 because they deal directly with prevention of the contamination of water. Parts L and M are excluded because they respectively address the conservation of fuel and power and access and facilities for disabled people. These matters are amongst the purposes, other than health and safety, that may be addressed by Building Regulations.

MATERIALS AND WORKMANSHIP

Any building work which is subject to the requirements imposed by Schedule 1 to the Building Regulations shall be carried out in accordance with regulation 7. Guidance on meeting these requirements on materials and workmanship is contained in Approved Document 7.

Building Regulations are made for specific purposes, primarily the health and safety, welfare and convenience of people and for energy conservation. Standards and other technical specifications may provide relevant guidance to the extent that they relate to these considerations. However, they may also address other aspects of performance or matters which, although they relate to health and safety etc., are not covered by the Building Regulations.

When an Approved Document makes reference to a named standard, the relevant version of the standard to which it refers is the one listed at the end of the publication. However, if this version has been revised or updated by the issuing standards body, the new version may be used as a source of guidance provided it continues to address the relevant requirements of the Regulations.

THE WORKPLACE (HEALTH, SAFETY AND WELFARE) REGULATIONS 1992

The Workplace (Health, Safety and Welfare) Regulations 1992 contain some requirements which affect building design. The main requirements are now covered by the Building Regulations, but for further information see *Workplace health, safety and welfare. Workplace (Health, Safety and Welfare) Regulations 1992. Approved Code of Practice L24.* Published by HSE Books 1992 (ISBN 0 7176 0413 6).

The Workplace (Health, Safety and Welfare) Regulations 1992 apply to the common parts of flats and similar buildings if people such as cleaners and caretakers are employed to work in these common parts. Where the requirements of the Building Regulations that are covered by this Part do not apply to dwellings, the provisions may still be required in the situations described above in order to satisfy the Workplace Regulations.

SAFE WORKING IN DRAINS AND SEWERS

Laying and maintaining drains are hazardous operations. Appropriate safety codes should be followed including procedures for working in confined spaces. Safe working procedures and permits to work may be required in some situations.

Relevant statutory requirements can be found in the Construction (Health, Safety and Welfare) Regulations 1996, SI 1996/1592, the Construction (Design and Management) Regulations 1994, SI 1994/3140 and the Confined Spaces Regulations 1997, SI 1997/1713.

The Health and Safety Executive operates an Information Line on 08701 545500, and produces the following advisory codes and information leaflets related to earthworks, drainage and working in confined spaces which are available from HSE Books, Tel 01787 881165.

Health and Safety in Excavation – be safe and shore, Booklet HSG 185.

Safe Work in Confined Spaces – Approved Code of Practice, Regulations and Guidance, Booklet L101.

The Requirement

This Approved Document, which took effect on 1 April 2002, deals with the following Requirement which is contained in the Building Regulations 2010

Requirement	Limits on application
Foul water drainage **H1.** (1) An adequate system of drainage shall be provided to carry foul water from appliances within the building to one of the following, listed in order of priority: (a) a public sewer; or, where that is not reasonably practicable, (b) a private sewer communicating with a public sewer; or, where that is not reasonably practicable, (c) either a septic tank which has an appropriate form of secondary treatment or another wastewater treatment system; or, where that is not reasonably practicable, (d) a cesspool. (2) In this Part 'foul water' means waste water which comprises or includes: (a) waste from a sanitary convenience, bidet or appliance used for washing receptacles for foul waste; or (b) water which has been used for food preparation, cooking or washing.	Requirement H1 does not apply to the diversion of water which has been used for personal washing or for the washing of clothes, linen or other articles to collection systems for re-use.

Guidance

Performance

In the Secretary of State's view the requirement of H1 will be met if a foul water drainage system:

a. conveys the flow of foul water to a foul water outfall (a foul or combined sewer, a cesspool, septic tank or holding tank);

b. minimises the risk of blockage or leakage;

c. prevents foul air from the drainage system from entering the building under working conditions;

d. is ventilated;

e. is accessible for clearing blockages; and

f. does not increase the vulnerability of the building to flooding.

Introduction to provisions

0.1 The capacity of the system should be large enough to carry the expected flow at any point.

0.2 The capacity depends on the size and gradient of the pipes. Minimum sizes and gradient limits are given in the text.

0.3 The pipe sizes quoted in this document are nominal sizes used as a numerical designation in convenient round numbers approximately equal to a manufacturer's size. Equivalent pipe sizes for individual pipe standards will be found in the standards listed in Tables 4, 7 and 14.

Section 1: Sanitary pipework

1.1 The provisions in this section are applicable to domestic buildings and small non-domestic buildings. Further guidance on larger buildings is given in Appendix A. Complex systems in larger buildings should be designed in accordance with BS EN 12056 (see paragraph 1.39).

1.2 The guidance in these provisions is applicable for WCs with major flush volumes of 5 litres or more. Where WCs with major flush volumes less than 5 litres are used, consideration should be given to the increased risk of blockages. Guidance on the design of sanitary pipework suitable for use with WCs with major flush volumes as low as 4 litres can be found in BS EN 12056 (see paragraph 1.39).

Traps

1.3 All points of discharge into the system should be fitted with a trap (e.g. a water seal trap) to prevent foul air from the system entering the building. Under working and test conditions traps should retain a minimum seal of 25mm of water or equivalent.

1.4 Table 1 gives minimum trap sizes and seal depths for the appliances which are most used (for other appliances see Appendix paragraph A4).

1.5 **Pressure fluctuation** – To prevent the water seal from being broken by the pressures which can develop in the system the branch discharge pipes should be designed as described in paragraphs 1.7 to 1.25.

1.6 **Access for clearing blockages** – If a trap forms part of an appliance the appliance should be removable. All other traps should be fitted directly after the appliance and should be removable or be fitted with a cleaning eye.

Table 1 Minimum trap sizes and seal depths

Appliance	Diameter of trap (mm)	Depth of seal (mm of water or equivalent)
Washbasin [1] Bidet	32	75
Bath [2] Shower [2]	40	50
Food waste disposal unit Urinal bowl Sink Washing machine [2] Dishwashing machine [2]	40	75
WC pan – outlet <80mm WC pan – outlet >80mm	75 100	50 50

[1] The depth of seal may be reduced to 50mm only with flush grated wastes without plugs on spray tap basins.

[2] Where these appliances discharge directly to a gully the depth of seal may be reduced to not less than 38mm.

[3] Traps used on appliances with flat bottom (trailing waste discharge) and discharging to a gully with a grating may have a reduced water seal of not less than 38mm.

Branch discharge pipes

1.7 Branch pipes should discharge into another branch pipe or a discharge stack unless the appliances discharge to a gully. Gullies are generally at ground floor level, but may be at basement level. Branch pipes should not discharge into open hoppers.

1.8 If the appliances are on the ground floor the pipe(s) may discharge to a stub stack or discharge stack, directly to a drain or (if the pipe carries only wastewater) to a gully. (See paragraphs 1.11 and 1.30.)

1.9 A branch pipe from a ground floor closet should only discharge directly to a drain if the depth from the floor to the drain is 1.3m or less (see Diagram 1).

Diagram 1 Direct connection of ground floor WC to a drain

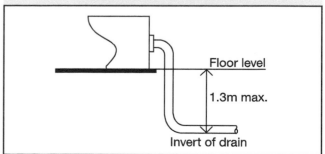

Floor level

1.3m max.

Invert of drain

Diagram 2 Branch connection to stacks – crossflow prevention

A branch creates a no connection zone on a stack
No other branch may be fitted such that its centre
line falls inside a zone but its centre line may be
on the boundary of the zone

Opposed branch connection in the
horizontal plane should be avoided

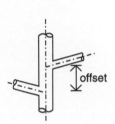

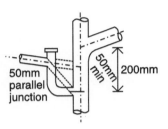

offset

lowest
connection

wc

A

B

450mm
min *

200mm

drain
invert

50mm
parallel
junction

50mm
min

200mm

Key

A opposed connections without
swept entries not exceeding 65mm
should be offset
110mm on a 100mm diameter stack
250mm on a 150mm diameter stack

Opposed connections larger than 65mm
(without swept entries) should be offset at
least 200mm irrespective of stack diameter
Unopposed connections may be at any position

B Angled connection or 50mm diameter
parallel junction where a branch discharge
pipe would enter the WC no connection
zone

NB A waste (branch discharge pipe)
manifold may be a suitable alternative

* This should be increased in buildings
over 3 storeys

1.10   A branch pipe should not discharge into a stack in a way which could cause crossflow into any other branch pipe. (See Diagram 2.)

1.11   A branch discharge pipe should not discharge into a stack lower than 450mm above the invert of the tail of the bend at the foot of the stack in single dwellings of up to 3 storeys (see Diagram 2). (For multi-storey buildings this should be increased, see Appendix paragraphs A5 and A6.)

1.12   Branch pipes may discharge into a stub stack. (See paragraph 1.30.)

1.13   A branch pipe discharging to a gully should terminate between the grating or sealing plate and the top of the water seal.

1.14   Condensate drainage from boilers may be connected to sanitary pipework. The connection should be made using pipework of minimum diameter 22mm through a 75mm condensate trap. If an additional trap is provided externally to the boiler to provide the 75mm seal, an air gap should be provided between the boiler and the trap.

a.   The connection should preferably be made to an internal stack with a 75mm condensate trap.

b.   If the connection is made to a branch pipe, the connection should be made downstream of any sink waste connection.

c.   All sanitary pipework receiving condensate should be made from materials resistant to a pH value of 6.5 and lower. The installation should be in accordance with BS 6798.

1.15   Sizes of branch pipes – Pipes serving a single appliance should have at least the same diameter as the appliance trap (see Table 1). If a pipe serves more than one appliance, and is unventilated, the diameter should be at least the size shown in Table 2.

1.16   Bends in branch pipes should be avoided if possible. Where they cannot they should have as large a radius as possible.

1.17   Junctions on branch pipes of about the same diameter should be made with a sweep of 25mm radius or at 45°. Connection of branch pipes of 75mm diameter or more to a stack of equal diameter should be made with a sweep of 50mm minimum radius or at 45°.

1.18   Branch pipes up to 40mm diameter joining branch pipes 100mm diameter or greater should, if practicable, connect to the upper part of the pipe wall of the larger branch.

1.19   Ventilation of branch pipes – separate ventilation will not be needed to prevent the water seals in traps from being lost by pressures which can develop in the system if the length and slope of the branch discharge pipes do not exceed those shown in Table 2 or Diagram 3.

Table 2 Common branch discharge pipes (unventilated)

Appliance	Max. no. to be connected	Max. length of branch pipe (m)	Min. size of pipe (mm)	Gradient limits (mm fall per metre)
WC outlet > 80mm	8	15	100	18[2] to 90
WC outlet < 80mm	1	15	75[3]	18 to 90
Urinal – bowl		3[1]	50	
Urinal – trough		3[1]	65	18 to 90
Urinal – slab		3[1]		
Washbasin or bidet	3	1.7	30	18 to 22
		1.1	30	18 to 44
		0.7	30	18 to 87
		3.0	40	18 to 44
	4	4.0	50	18 to 44

[1] Should be as short as possible to prevent deposition.

[2] May be reduced to 9mm on long drain runs where space is restricted, but only if more than one WC is connected.

[3] Not recommended where disposal of sanitary towels may take place via the WC, as there is an increased risk of blockages.

[4] Slab urinals longer than seven persons should have more than one outlet.

Diagram 3 Branch connections

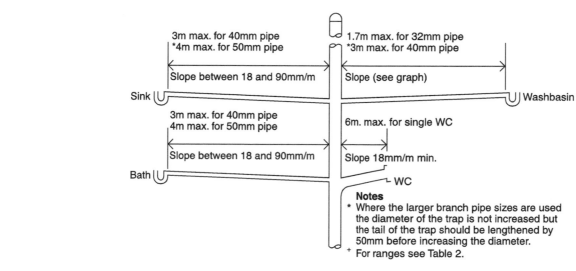

(a) Unvented branch connections to stacks

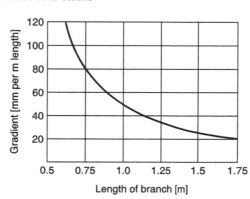

(b) Design curve for 32mm washbasin waste pipes

1.20   If the figures in Table 2 and Diagram 3 are exceeded the branch pipe should be ventilated by a branch ventilating pipe to external air, to a ventilating stack (ventilated branch system) or internally by use of an air admittance valve.

1.21   A separate ventilating stack is only likely to be preferred where the numbers of sanitary appliances and their distance to a discharge stack are large. (See Appendix paragraphs A7 to A9.)

1.22   Branch ventilating pipes – should be connected to the discharge pipe within 750mm of the trap and should connect to the ventilating stack or the stack vent, above the highest 'spillover' level of the appliances served (see Diagram 4). The ventilating pipe should have a continuous incline from the discharge pipe to the point of connection to the ventilating stack or stack vent.

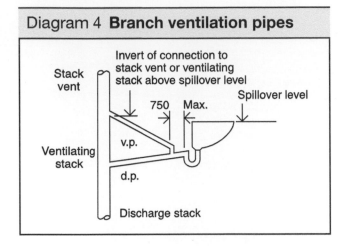

Diagram 4 Branch ventilation pipes

1.23   Branch ventilating pipes which run direct to outside air should finish at least 900mm above any opening into the building nearer than 3m (see Diagram 6 and paragraph 1.31).

1.24   Branch ventilating pipes to branch pipes serving one appliance should be at least 25mm diameter or where the branch is longer than 15m or has more than 5 bends, should be at least 32mm.

1.25   Rodding points should be provided to give access to any lengths of discharge pipe which cannot be reached by removing traps or appliances with internal traps (see paragraph 1.6).

Discharge stacks

1.26   All stacks should discharge to a drain. The bend at the foot of the stack should have as large a radius as possible and at least 200mm at the centre line.

1.27   Offsets in the 'wet' portion of a discharge stack should be avoided. If they are unavoidable then in a building of not more than 3 storeys there should be no branch connection within 750mm of the offset. In a building over 3 storeys a ventilation stack may be needed with connections above and below the offset. In buildings over

3 storeys discharge stacks should be located inside the building.

1.28   Sizes of stacks – Stacks should have at least the diameter shown in Table 3 and should not reduce in the direction of flow. Stacks serving urinals should be not less than 50mm, stacks serving closets with outlets less than 80mm should be not less than 75mm and stacks serving closets with outlets greater than 80mm should be not less than 100mm. The internal diameter of the stack should be not less than that of the largest trap or branch discharge pipe. For larger buildings the maximum flow should be checked. (See paragraphs A.1 to A.3.)

Table 3 Minimum diameters for discharge stacks

Stack size (mm)	Max. capacity (litres/sec)
50*	1.2
65*	2.1
75†	3.4
90	5.3
100	7.2

Notes:

*   No WCs.

†   Not more than 1 WC with outlet size <80mm.

1.29   Ventilation of discharge stacks – To prevent water seals in the traps from being lost by pressures which can develop in the system, discharge stacks should be ventilated. Discharge stacks connected to drains liable to surcharging or near an intercepting trap require ventilating pipes of not less than 50mm diameter connected to the base of the stack above the likely flood level.

1.30   Stub stacks – A stub stack may be used if it connects into a ventilated discharge stack or into a ventilated drain not subject to surcharging and no connected water closet has a floor level more than 1.3m and no other branch into the stub stack has a centreline more than 2m to the centre line above the invert of the connection or drain (see Diagram 5).

Diagram 5 **Stub stack**

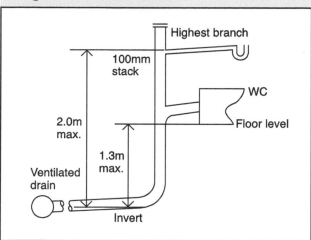

Diagram 6 **Termination of ventilation stacks or ventilation part of discharge**

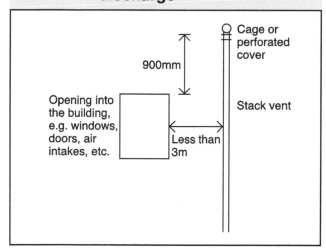

1.31 Ventilating pipes open to outside air should finish at least 900mm above any opening into the building within 3m and should be finished with a wire cage or other perforated cover, fixed to the end of the ventilating pipe, which does not restrict the flow of air (see Diagram 6). In areas where rodent control is a problem (see paragraph 2.22) these should be metallic.

1.32   Sizes of stack ventilation pipes – stack ventilation pipes (the dry part above the highest branch) may be reduced in size in one and two storey houses, but should be not less than 75mm.

1.33 Ventilated discharge stacks may be terminated inside a building when fitted with air admittance valves complying with BS EN 12380:2002. Where these valves are used they should not adversely affect the amount of ventilation necessary for the below ground system which is normally provided by open stacks of the sanitary pipework. Air admittance valves should be located in areas which have

adequate ventilation, should be accessible for maintenance and should be removable to give access for clearance of blockages. Air admittance valves should not be used outside buildings or in dust laden atmospheres. Where there is no open ventilation on a drainage system or through connected drains, alternative arrangements to relieve positive pressures should be considered.

1.34   Access for clearing blockages – rodding points should be provided in discharge stacks to give access to any lengths of pipe which cannot be reached from any other part of the system. All pipes should be reasonably accessible for repair. Rodding points in stacks should be above the spillover level of appliances.

Materials for pipes, fittings and joints

1.35 Any of the materials shown in Table 4 may be used (the references are to British Standard or European Standard Specifications). Where necessary different metals should be separated by non-metallic material to prevent electrolytic corrosion. Care should be taken to ensure continuity of any electrical earth bonding requirements. Pipes should be firmly supported without restricting thermal movement. *Attention is also drawn to the requirement of Part B of Schedule 1 to the Building Regulations 2000 and guidance in the Approved Document relating to penetration of fire separating elements and fire stopping provisions.*

Table 4	**Materials for sanitary pipework**
Material	**British Standard**
Pipes	
Cast iron	BS 416, BS EN 877
Copper	BS EN 1254, BS EN 1057
Galvanised steel	BS 3868
PVC-U	BS EN 1329
Polypropylene (PP)	BS EN 1451
ABS	BS EN 1455
Polyethylene (PE)	BS EN 1519
Styrene copolymer blends (PVC + SAN)	BS EN 1565
PVC-C	BS EN 1566
Traps	BS EN 274, BS 3943

Note: Some of these materials may not be suitable for carrying trade effluent or condensate from boilers.

1.36 Sanitary pipework connected to WCs should not allow light to be visible through the pipe wall, as this is believed to encourage damage by rodents.

Workmanship

1.37   Good workmanship is essential.
Workmanship should be in accordance with
BS 8000 *Workmanship on Building Sites* Part 13:
Code of practice for above ground drainage.

Air tightness

1.38   The pipes, fittings and joints should be
capable of withstanding an air test of positive
pressure of at least 38mm water gauge for at
least 3 minutes. Every trap should maintain a
water seal of at least 25mm. Smoke testing may
be used to identify defects where a water test
has failed. Smoke testing is not recommended
for PVC-U pipes.

Alternative approach

1.39   The requirement can also be met by
following the relevant recommendations of
BS EN 12056 *Gravity drainage systems inside
buildings*. Relevant clauses are in Part 1: *General
and performance requirements*, Clauses 3–6;
Part 2 *Sanitary pipework, layout and calculation*,
Clauses 3 to 6 and National Annexes NA to NG
(System III is traditionally in use in the UK); Part 5
*Installation and testing, instructions for operation,
maintenance and use*, Clauses 4–6, 8, 9 and 11.
BS EN 12109 *Vacuum Drainage Systems
Inside Buildings.*

Section 2: Foul drainage

2.1 This section gives guidance on the construction of underground drains and sewers from buildings to the point of connection to an existing sewer or a cesspool or wastewater treatment system and includes any drains or sewers outside the curtilage of the building. Disused and defective pipework is known to harbour rats (see Appendix H1-B).

2.2 Some public sewers may carry foul water and rainwater in the same pipes. If the drainage system is also to carry rainwater to such a sewer, the following provisions still apply but the pipe sizes may need to be increased to carry the combined flows (see paragraph 2.35). In some circumstances, separate drainage should still be provided (see Approved Document H5).

Outlets

2.3 Foul drainage should be connected to a public foul or combined sewer wherever this is reasonably practicable. For small developments connection should be made to a public sewer where this is within 30m provided that the developer has the right to construct the drainage over any intervening private land. Where levels do not permit drainage by gravity a pumping installation should be provided (see paragraphs 2.36 to 2.39).

2.4 For larger developments it may be economic to connect to a public sewer even where the sewer is some distance away. For developments comprising more than one curtilage, the developer may requisition a sewer from the sewerage undertaker who has powers to construct sewers over private land (see Appendix H1-C, C.4).

2.5 The sewerage undertaker should be notified at least three weeks before it is intended to connect to the public sewer (see Appendix H1-C, C.7).

2.6 Where it is not reasonably practicable to connect to a public sewer, it may be possible to connect to an existing private sewer that connects with a public sewer. The permission of the owner or owners of the sewer will be required. The sewer should be in satisfactory condition and have sufficient capacity to take the additional flows.

2.7 Where none of these options is reasonably practicable, a wastewater treatment system or cesspool should be provided (see Approved Document H2).

Surcharging of drains

2.8 Combined and rainwater sewers are designed to surcharge (i.e. the water level in the manhole rises above the top of the pipe) in heavy rainfall. Some foul sewers also receive rainwater and therefore surcharge. For low-lying sites (where the ground level of the site or the level of a basement is below the ground level at the point where the drainage connects to the public sewer) care should be taken to ensure that the property is not at increased risk of flooding. In all such cases the sewerage undertaker should be consulted to determine the extent and possible frequency of the likely surcharge.

2.9 For basements containing sanitary appliances, where the risk of flooding due to surcharge of the sewer is considered by the sewerage undertaker to be high, the drainage from the basement should be pumped (see paragraphs 2.36 to 2.39). Where the risk is considered to be low an anti-flooding valve should be installed on the drainage from the basement.

2.10 For other low-lying sites (i.e. not basements) where risk is considered low, sufficient protection for the building may be possible by provision of a gully outside the building at least 75mm below the floor level. This should be positioned so that any flooding from the gully will not damage any buildings. In higher risk areas an anti-flooding valve should be provided, or the drainage system pumped (see paragraph 2.36 to 2.39).

2.11 Anti-flooding valves should preferably be of the double valve type, and should be suitable for foul water and have a manual closure device. They should comply with the requirements of prEN 13564. A single valve should not normally serve more than one building. A notice should be provided inside the building to indicate that the system is drained through such a valve. This notice should also indicate the location of any manual override, and include advice on necessary maintenance.

2.12 All drainage unaffected by surcharge should by-pass the protective measures and discharge by gravity.

Layout

2.13 The layout of the drainage system should be kept simple. Changes of direction and gradient should be minimised and as easy as practicable. Access points should be provided only if blockages could not be cleared without them.

2.14 Connection of drains to other drains or private or public sewers, and of private sewers to public sewers, should be made obliquely, or in the direction of flow.

2.15 Connections should be made using prefabricated components. Where holes are cut in pipes a drilling device should be used to avoid damaging the pipe.

2.16 Where connections made to existing drains or sewers involve removal of pipes and insertion of a junction, repair couplings should be used to ensure a watertight joint and the junction should be carefully packed to avoid differential settlement with adjacent pipes.

2.17 Sewers (serving more than one property) should be kept as far as is practicable away from the point on a building where a future extension is likely (e.g. rear of a house, or side of house where there is room for a side extension).

2.18 The system should be ventilated by a flow of air. A ventilating pipe should be provided at or near the head of each main drain. An open ventilating pipe (without an air admittance valve) should be provided on any drain fitted with an intercepting trap (particularly on a sealed system), and on any drain subject to surcharge. Ventilated discharge stacks may be used (see paragraphs 1.27 and 1.29). Ventilating pipes should not finish near openings in buildings (see paragraph 1.31).

2.19 Pipes should be laid to even gradients and any change of gradient should be combined with an access point (see paragraph 2.49).

2.20 Pipes should also be laid in straight lines where practicable but may be laid to slight curves if these can still be cleared of blockages. Any bends should be limited to positions in or close to inspection chambers or manholes (see paragraph 2.49) and to the foot of discharge and ventilating stacks. Bends should have as large a radius as practicable.

2.21 Drainage serving kitchens in commercial hot food premises should be fitted with a grease separator complying with BS EN 1825-1:2004 and designed in accordance with BS EN 1825-2:2002 or other effective means of grease removal.

Special protection – rodent control

2.22 Where the site has been previously developed the local authority should be consulted to determine whether any special measures are necessary for control of rodents. Special measures which may be taken include the following.

a. Sealed drainage – drainage having access covers to the pipework in the inspection chamber instead of an open channel. These should only be used in inspection chambers, where maintenance can be carried out from the surface without personnel entry.

b. Intercepting traps – These are susceptible to blockage and require frequent maintenance. Intercepting trap stoppers should be of the locking type that can be easily removed from the chamber surface and securely replaced after blockage clearance. It is important that stoppers are replaced after maintenance. These should only be used in inspection chambers where maintenance can be carried out from the surface without personnel entry.

c. Rodent barriers – a number of rodent barrier devices are used in other countries; these include: enlarged sections on discharge stacks to prevent rats climbing, flexible downward facing fins in the discharge stack, or one way valves in underground drainage.

d. Metal cages on ventilator stack terminals should also be used to discourage rats from leaving the drainage system (see paragraph 1.31).

e. Covers and gratings to gullies may be displaced or attacked by rats. Solid plastic covers or metal gratings which can be fixed in place should be used to discourage rats from leaving the system.

Protection from settlement

2.23 A drain may run under a building if at least 100mm of granular or other flexible filling is provided round the pipe. On sites where excessive subsidence is possible additional flexible joints may be advisable or other solutions such as suspended drainage, particularly where the pipe is adjacent to structures or where soil conditions change in the course of the pipe run. Where the crown of the pipe is within 300mm of the underside of the slab, special protection should be provided (see paragraph 2.44).

2.24 At any points where pipes are built into a structure, including an inspection chamber, manhole, footing, ground beam or wall, suitable measures should be taken to prevent damage or misalignment. This may be achieved by either:

a. building in a length of pipe (as short as possible) with its joints as close as possible to the wall faces (within at most 150mm) and connected on each side of rocker pipes by a length of at most 600mm and flexible joints (see Diagram 7(a)); or

b. forming an opening to give at least 50mm clearance all round the pipe and the opening masked with rigid sheet material to prevent ingress of fill or vermin. It is important that the void is also filled with a compressible sealant to prevent ingress of gas (see Diagram 7(b)).

2.25 A drain trench should not be excavated lower than the foundations of any building nearby (see Diagram 8) unless either:

a. where the trench is within 1m of the foundation the trench is filled with concrete up to the lowest level of the foundation; or

b. where the trench is further than 1m from the building, the trench is filled with concrete to a level below the lowest level for the building equal to the distance from the building, less 150mm.

Diagram 7 Pipes penetrating walls

(a) Short length of pipe bedded in wall, joints formed within 150mm of either wallface. Adjacent rocker pipes of max. length 600mm with flexible joints

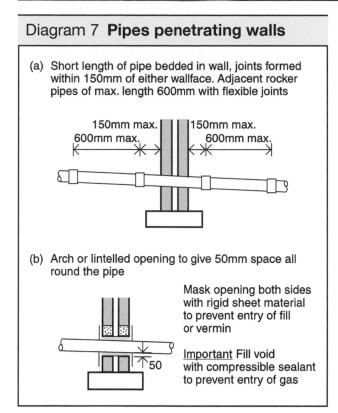

(b) Arch or lintelled opening to give 50mm space all round the pipe

Mask opening both sides with rigid sheet material to prevent entry of fill or vermin

Important Fill void with compressible sealant to prevent entry of gas

Diagram 8 Pipe runs near buildings

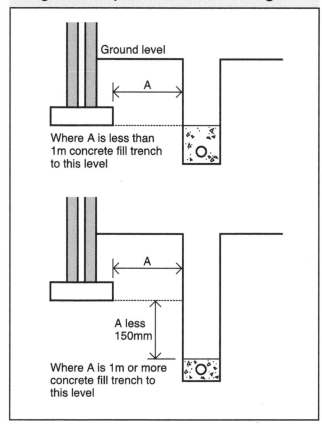

Ground level

A

Where A is less than 1m concrete fill trench to this level

A

A less 150mm

Where A is 1m or more concrete fill trench to this level

2.26 Where pipes are to be laid on piles or beams or in a common trench, or where the ground may prove unstable particularly where there is a high water table, advice may be found in TRL *A guide to the design loadings for buried rigid pipes*. The local authority may be able to provide information regarding the site.

Depth of pipe cover

2.27 The depth of cover will usually depend on the levels of the connections to the system, the gradients at which the pipes should be laid and the ground levels.

2.28 Pipes also need to be protected from damage and if the limits of cover are not attainable it may be possible to choose another pipe strength and pipe bedding class combination (Guidance is given in BS EN 1295-1 National Annex NA). Alternatively special protection can be provided (see paragraphs 2.41 to 2.45).

Pipe gradients and sizes

2.29 Drains should have enough capacity to carry the flow. The flow depends on the appliances connected (see paragraphs 0.1–0.3 and Table 5) and the capacity depends on the size and gradient of the pipes (see Diagram 9).

Diagram 9 Discharge capacities of foul drains running 0.75 proportional depth

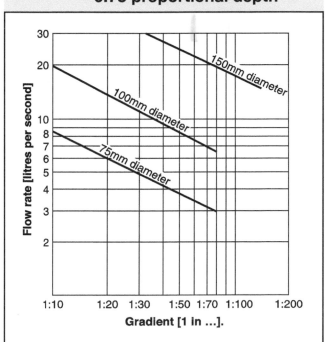

Table 5 Flow rates from dwellings

Number of dwellings	Flow rate (litres/sec)
1	2.5
5	3.5
10	4.1
15	4.6
20	5.1
25	5.4
30	5.8

2.30 Sewers (i.e. a drain serving more than one property) should normally have a minimum diameter of 100mm when serving no more than 10 dwellings. Sewers serving more than 10 dwellings should normally have a minimum diameter of 150mm. See also Table C1.

2.31 The flow depends on the type, number and grouping of appliances.

2.32 Appliances are seldom in use simultaneously and the minimum drain sizes in normal use are capable of carrying the flow from quite large numbers of appliances. Table 5 shows approximate flow rates resulting from the typical household group of 1 WC, 1 bath, 1 or 2 washbasins, 1 sink and 1 washing machine used for design purposes in BS EN 12056.

2.33 A drain carrying foul water should have an internal diameter of at least 75mm. A drain carrying effluent from a WC or trade effluent should have an internal diameter of at least 100mm.

2.34 Table 6 shows the flattest gradients at which drains should be laid (depending on the flow and the appliances connected to them) and the capacity they will then have (see also paragraphs 0.1–0.3).

Table 6 Recommended minimum gradients for foul drains

Peak flow (litres/sec)	Pipe size (mm)	Minimum gradient (1 in ...)	Maximum capacity (litres/sec)
< 1	75	1:40	4.1
	100	1:40	9.2
> 1	75	1:80	2.8
	100	1:80*	6.3
	150	1:150†	15.0

Notes:
* Minimum of 1 WC
† Minimum of 5 WCs

2.35 Combined systems – the capacity of systems carrying foul water and rainwater should take account of the combined peak flow (see Approved Document H3 Rainwater drainage paragraph 3.8).

Pumping installations

2.36 Where gravity drainage is impracticable, or protection against flooding due to surcharge in downstream sewers is required, a pumping installation will be needed.

2.37 Package pumping installations are available which are suitable for installation within buildings. Floor mounted units may be particularly suited for installation in basements. These should conform to BS EN 12050. Pumping installations for use inside buildings should be designed in accordance with BS EN 12056-4.

2.38 Package pumping installations suitable for installation outside buildings are also available. Guidance on the design of pumping installations for use outside buildings may be found in BS EN 752-6.

2.39 Where foul water drainage from a building is to be pumped, the effluent receiving chamber should be sized to contain 24-hour inflow to allow for disruption in service. The minimum daily discharge of foul drainage should be taken as 150 litres per head per day for domestic use. For other types of building, the capacity of the receiving chamber should be based on the calculated daily demand of the water intake for the building. Where only a proportion of the foul sewage is to be pumped, then the capacity should be based pro-rata. In all pumped systems the controls should be so arranged to optimise pump operation.

Materials for pipes and jointing

Table 7 Materials for below ground gravity drainage

Material	British Standard
Rigid pipes	
Vitrified clay	BS 65, BS EN 295
Concrete	BS 5911
Grey iron	BS 437
Ductile iron	BS EN 598
Flexible pipes	
UPVC	BS EN 1401+
PP	BS EN 1852+
Structure walled plastic pipes	BS EN 13476

+ Application area code UD should normally be specified

Note: Some of these materials may not be suitable for conveying trade effluent

2.40 Any of the materials shown in Table 7 may be used (the references are to British Standard Specifications). Joints should be appropriate to the material of the pipes. To minimise the effects of any differential settlement pipes should have flexible joints. All joints should remain watertight under working and test conditions and nothing in the pipes, joints or fittings should project into the pipe line or cause an obstruction. Different metals should be separated by non-metallic materials to prevent electrolytic corrosion.

Bedding and backfilling

2.41 The choice of bedding and backfilling depends on the depth at which the pipes are to be laid and the size and strength of the pipes.

2.42 Rigid pipes – The types of bedding and backfilling which should be used for rigid pipes of standard strength laid in a trench of any width are shown in Diagram 10 and Tables 8 and 9. Minimum and maximum depths of cover are also shown for each type.

2.43 Flexible pipes – These will become deformed under load and require support to limit the deformation. The bedding and backfilling should be as shown in Diagram 10. Minimum and maximum depths of cover are also shown in Table 10.

2.44 Where pipes have less than the minimum recommended cover in Table 8, 9 or 10, the pipes should, where necessary, be protected from damage by a reinforced concrete cover slab with a

Diagram 10 Bedding for pipes

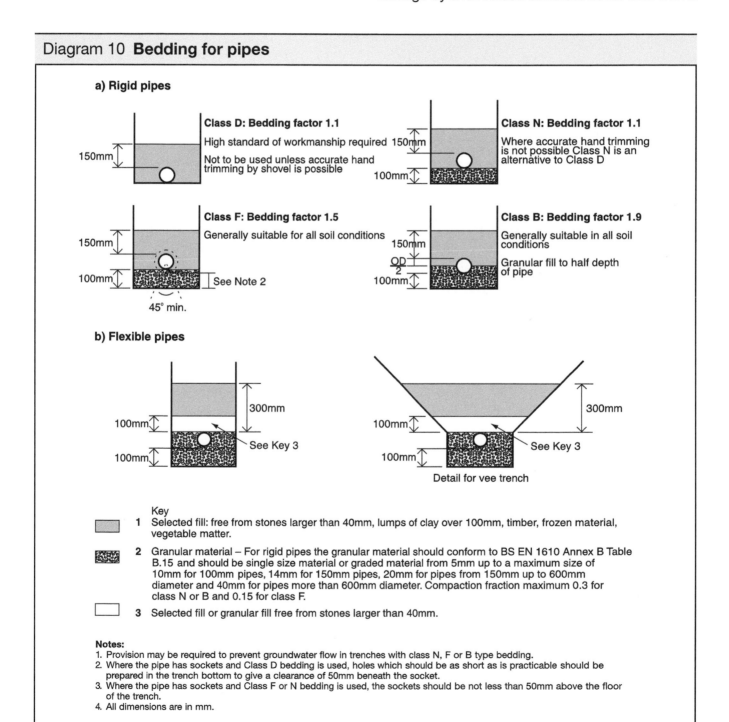

a) Rigid pipes

Class D: Bedding factor 1.1
High standard of workmanship required
Not to be used unless accurate hand trimming by shovel is possible

150mm

Class N: Bedding factor 1.1
Where accurate hand trimming is not possible Class N is an alternative to Class D

150mm
100mm

Class F: Bedding factor 1.5
Generally suitable for all soil conditions

150mm
100mm
See Note 2
45° min.

Class B: Bedding factor 1.9
Generally suitable in all soil conditions
Granular fill to half depth of pipe

150mm
$\frac{OD}{2}$
100mm

b) Flexible pipes

300mm
100mm
100mm
See Key 3

Detail for vee trench
300mm
100mm
100mm
See Key 3

Key

1. Selected fill: free from stones larger than 40mm, lumps of clay over 100mm, timber, frozen material, vegetable matter.

2. Granular material – For rigid pipes the granular material should conform to BS EN 1610 Annex B Table B.15 and should be single size material or graded material from 5mm up to a maximum size of 10mm for 100mm pipes, 14mm for 150mm pipes, 20mm for pipes from 150mm up to 600mm diameter and 40mm for pipes more than 600mm diameter. Compaction fraction maximum 0.3 for class N or B and 0.15 for class F.

3. Selected fill or granular fill free from stones larger than 40mm.

Notes:
1. Provision may be required to prevent groundwater flow in trenches with class N, F or B type bedding.
2. Where the pipe has sockets and Class D bedding is used, holes which should be as short as is practicable should be prepared in the trench bottom to give a clearance of 50mm beneath the socket.
3. Where the pipe has sockets and Class F or N bedding is used, the sockets should be not less than 50mm above the floor of the trench.
4. All dimensions are in mm.

flexible filler and at least 75mm of granular material between the top of the pipe and the underside of the flexible filler below the slabs (see Diagram 11 and paragraphs 2.28, 2.42 and 2.43).

2.45   Where it is necessary to backfill the trench with concrete in order to protect nearby foundations (see paragraph 2.25) movement joints formed with compressible board should be provided at each socket or sleeve joint face (see Diagram 12).

Table 8 Limits of cover for class 120 clayware pipes in any width of trench

Nominal size	Laid in fields	Laid in light roads	Laid in main roads
100mm	0.6m – 8+m	1.2m – 8+m	1.2m – 8m
225mm	0.6m – 5m	1.2m – 5m	1.2m – 4.5m
400mm	0.6m – 4.5m	1.2m – 4.5m	1.2m – 4m
600mm	0.6m – 4.5m	1.2m – 4.5m	1.2m – 4m

Notes:

1.   All pipes assumed to be Class 120 to BS EN 295; other strengths and sizes of pipe are available, consult manufacturers.

2.   Bedding assumed to be Class B with bedding factor of 1.9; guidance is available on use of higher bedding factors with clayware pipes.

3.   Alternative designs using different pipe strengths and/or bedding types may offer more appropriate or economic options using the procedures set out in BS EN 1295.

4.   Minimum depth in roads set to 1.2m irrespective of pipe strength.

Table 9 Limits of cover for class M concrete pipes in any width of trench

Nominal size	Laid in fields	Laid in light roads	Laid in main roads
300mm	0.6m – 3m	1.2m – 3m	1.2m – 2.5m
450mm	0.6m – 3.5m	1.2m – 3.5m	1.2m – 2.5m
600mm	0.6m – 3.5m	1.2m – 3.5m	1.2m – 3m

Notes:

1.   All pipes assumed to be Class M to BS 5911; other strengths and sizes of pipe are available, consult manufacturers.

2.   Bedding assumed to be Class B with bedding factor of 1.9.

3.   Alternative designs using different pipe strengths and/or bedding types may offer more appropriate or economic options using the procedures set out in BS EN 1295.

4.   Minimum depth in roads set to 1.2m irrespective of pipe strength.

Table 10 Limits of cover for thermoplastics (nominal ring stiffness SN4) pipes in any width of trench

Nominal size	Laid in fields	Laid in light roads	Laid in main roads
100mm – 300mm	0.6m – 7m	0.9m – 7m	0.9m – 7m

Notes:

1.   For drains and sewers less than 1.5m deep and there is a risk of excavation adjacent to the drain and depth, special calculation is necessary, see BS EN 1295.

2.   All pipes assumed to be to in accordance with the relevant standard listed in Table 7 with nominal ring stiffness SN4; other strengths and sizes of pipe are available, consult manufacturers.

3.   Bedding assumed to be Class S2 with 80% compaction and average soil conditions.

4.   Alternative designs using different pipe strengths and/or bedding types may offer more appropriate or economic options using the procedures set out in BS EN 1295.

5.   Minimum depth is set to 1.5m irrespective of pipe strength to cover loss of side support from parallel excavations.

Diagram 11 **Protection for pipes laid at shallow depths (minimum sizes)**

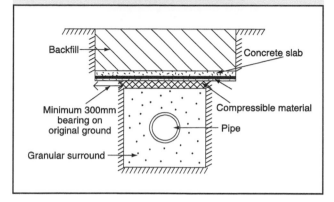

Diagram 12 **Joints for concrete encased pipes (minimum sizes)**

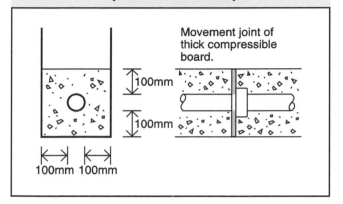

Clearance of blockages

2.46 Sufficient and suitable access points should be provided for clearing blockages from drain runs which cannot be reached by any other means. The siting, spacing and type of the access points will depend on the layout, depth and size of the runs.

2.47 The provisions described below are for normal methods of rodding (which need not be in the direction of flow) and not mechanical means of clearing.

2.48 Access points should be one of four types. Tables 11 and 12 show the depth at which each type should be used and the recommended dimensions it should have. The dimensions should be increased at junctions if they do not allow enough space for branches. The types are:

a. rodding eyes – capped extensions of the pipes;

b. access fittings – small chambers on (or an extension of) the pipes but not with an open channel;

c. inspection chambers – chambers with working space at ground level;

d. manholes – deep chambers with working space at drain level.

2.49 Siting of access points – access should be provided at the following points:

a. on or near the head of each drain run, and

b. at a bend and at a change of gradient, and

c. at a change of pipe size (but see below if it is at a junction), and

d. at a junction unless each run can be cleared from an access point (some junctions can only be rodded through from one direction).

Table 11 **Minimum dimensions for access fittings and inspection chambers**

Type	Depth to invert from cover level (m)	Internal sizes		Cover sizes	
		Length x width (mm x mm)	Circular (mm)	Length x width (mm x mm)	Circular (mm)
Rodding eye		As drain but min. 100			Same size as pipework [1]
Access fitting small	150 diam. 150 x 100	0.6 or less, except where	150 x 100	150	150 x 100 [1]	Same size as
large	225 x 100	situated in a chamber	225 x 100	225	225 x 100 [1]	access fitting
Inspection chamber shallow	0.6 or less	225 x 100	190 [2]	–	190 [1]
	1.2 or less	450 x 450	450	Min. 430 x 430	430
deep	> 1.2	450 x 450	450	Max. 300 x 300 [3]	Access restricted to max. 350 [3]

Notes:

1. The clear opening may be reduced by 20mm in order to provide proper support for the cover and frame.

2. Drains up to 150mm.

3. A larger clear opening cover may be used in conjunction with a restricted access. The size is restricted for health and safety reasons to deter entry.

Table 12 Minimum dimensions for manholes

Type	Size of largest pipe (DN)	Min. internal dimensions [1]		Min. clear opening size [1]	
		Rectangular length and width	Circular diameter	Rectangular length and width	Circular diameter
Manhole					
< 1.5m deep to soffit	≤ 150	750 x 675 [7]	1000 [7]	750 x 675 [2]	na [3]
	225	1200 x 675	1200	1200 x 675 [2]	
	300	1200 x 750	1200		
	>300	1800 x (DN+450)	The larger of 1800 or (DN+450)		
>1.5m deep to soffit	≤ 225	1200 x 1000	1200	600 x 600	600
	300	1200 x 1075	1200		
	375-450	1350 x 1225	1200		
	>450	1800 x (DN+775)	The larger of 1800 or (DN+775)		
Manhole shaft [4]					
> 3.0m deep to	Steps [5]	1050 x 800	1050	600 x 600	600
soffit of pipe	Ladder [5]	1200 x 800	1200		
	Winch [6]	900 x 800	900	600 x 600	600

Notes:

1. Larger sizes may be required for manholes on bends or where there are junctions.
2. May be reduced to 600 by 600 where required by highway loading considerations, subject to a safe system of work being specified.
3. Not applicable due to working space needed.
4. Minimum height of chamber in shafted manhole 2m from benching to underside of reducing slab.
5. Min. clear space between ladder or steps and the opposite face of the shaft should be approximately 900mm.
6. Winch only – no steps or ladders, permanent or removable.
7. The minimum size of any manhole serving a sewer (i.e. any drain serving more than one property) should be 1200mm x 675mm rectangular or 1200mm diameter.

2.50 Access should be provided to long runs. The distances between access points depend on the types of access used but should not be more than shown in Table 13 for drains up to and including 300mm.

2.51 Access points to sewers (serving more than one property) should be in places where they are accessible and apparent for use in an emergency. Examples of suitable locations include highways, public open space, unfenced front gardens and shared or unfenced driveways.

2.52 **Construction of access points** – these should contain the foul water under working and test conditions and resist the entry of groundwater and rainwater. Any of the materials shown in Table 14 may be used.

2.53 Where half round channels are used in inspection chambers and manholes the branches up to and including 150mm diameter should discharge into the channel in the direction of flow at or above the level of the horizontal diameter. A branch with a diameter >150mm should be set with the soffit level with that of the main drain. Where the angle of the branch is more than 45° a three quarter section branch should be used. Channels and branches should be benched up at least to the top of the outgoing pipe and at a slope of 1 in 12. The benching should be rounded at the channel with a radius of at least 25mm.

Table 13 Maximum spacing of access points in metres

From	To Access Fitting		To Junction	To Inspection chamber	To Manhole
	Small	Large			
Start of external drain [1]	12	12	–	22	45
Rodding eye	22	22	22	45	45
Access fitting: small 150 diam. and 150 x 100 large 225 x 100	– –	– –	12 22	22 45	22 45
Inspection chamber shallow	22	45	22	45	45
Manhole and inspection chamber deep	–	–	–	45	90 [2]

Notes:

1. Stack or ground floor appliance

2. May be up to 200 for man-entry size drains and sewers

Table 14 Materials for access points

Material	British Standard
1. **Inspection chambers and manholes** Clay, bricks and blocks Vitrified clay Concrete – precast Concrete – in situ Plastics	 BS 3921 BS EN 295, BS 65 BS 5911 BS 8110 BS 7158
2. **Rodding eyes and access fittings** (excluding frames and covers)	 as pipes see Table 7 ETA Certificates

2.54 Inspection chambers and manholes should have removable non-ventilating covers of durable material (such as cast iron, cast or pressed steel, precast concrete or plastics) and be of suitable strength. Small lightweight access covers should be secured (for example with screws) to deter unauthorised access (for example by children). Inspection chambers and manholes in buildings should have mechanically fixed airtight covers unless the drain itself has watertight access covers. Manholes deeper than 1m should have metal step irons or fixed ladders.

Workmanship

2.55 Good workmanship is essential. Workmanship should be in accordance with BS 8000 *Workmanship on Building Sites* Part 14: *Code of practice for below ground drainage.*

2.56 During construction, drains and sewers which are left open should be covered when work is not in progress to prevent entry by rats.

2.57 Any drain or sewer should be protected from damage by construction traffic and heavy machinery. Protection may be provided by providing barriers to keep such traffic away from the line of the sewer. Heavy materials should not be stored over drains or sewers.

2.58 Where piling works are being carried out care should be taken to avoid damage to any drain or sewer. The position of the drain or sewer should be established by survey. If the drain or sewer is within 1m of the piling, trial holes should be excavated to establish the exact position of the sewer. The location of any connections should also be established. Piling should not be carried out where the distance from the outside of the sewer to the outside of the pile is less than two times the diameter of the pile.

Testing and inspection

2.59 **Water tightness** – after laying, including any necessary concrete or other haunching or surrounding and backfilling, gravity drains and private sewers should be tested for water tightness using either an air test or a water test. Information on test requirements is given in paragraphs 2.60 and 2.61 for pipe sizes up to 300mm. For further information and for larger sizes see BS 8000 Part 14 or BS EN 1610.

2.60 **Air test** – for pipes up to 300mm diameter, the pipe should be pressurised up to a pressure of 110mm water gauge and held for approximately 5 minutes prior to testing. Following this the pipe should be able to hold an initial 100mm pressure with a maximum loss of head on a manometer of 25mm in a period of 7 minutes.

2.61　Water test – For pipes up to 300mm diameter the system should be filled with water up to a depth of 5m above the lowest invert in the test section and a minimum depth of 1m measured at the highest invert in the test section. This may then be left for a period (one hour is generally sufficient) to condition the pipe. The test pressure should then be maintained for a period of 30 minutes, by topping up the water level as necessary so that it is within 100mm of the required level throughout the test. The losses per square metre of surface area should not exceed 0.15 litres for test lengths with only pipelines or 0.20 litres for test lengths including pipelines and manholes, or 0.40 litres for tests with only manholes and inspection chambers alone (i.e. no pipelines).

2.62　Connectivity – Where separate drainage systems are provided (see Approved Document H5), connections should be proven to ensure that they are connected to the correct system.

Alternative approach

2.63　The requirement can also be met by following the relevant recommendations of BS EN 752. The relevant clauses are in Part 3, Part 4 and Part 6. BS EN 752, together with BS EN 1610 and BS EN 1295, contains additional information about design and construction. BS EN 12056 describes the discharge unit method of calculating flows. Also by providing systems meeting the requirements of BS EN 1091 *Vacuum sewerage systems outside buildings*, or BS EN 1671 *Pressure sewerage systems outside buildings*.

Appendix H1-A: Additional guidance for larger buildings

Capacity of pipes

(see paragraph 1.28)

A.1 The flow depends on the type, number and grouping of appliances.

A.2 Appliances are seldom in use simultaneously and the minimum stack sizes in normal use are capable of carrying the flow from quite large numbers of appliances. Table A1 shows approximate flow rates resulting from the typical household group of 1 WC, 1 bath, 1 or 2 washbasins, 1 sink and 1 washing machine used for design purposes in BS EN 12056.

Table A1 Flow rates from dwellings

Number of dwellings	Flow rate (litres/sec)
1	2.5
5	3.5
10	4.1
15	4.6
20	5.1
25	5.4
30	5.8

A.3 Flow rates for other commonly used appliances not covered in Table A1 are shown in Table A2.

Table A2 Flow rates from appliances

Appliance	Flow rate (litres/sec)
Spray tap basin	0.06
Washing machine	0.70
Dishwashing machine	0.25
Urinal (per person)	0.15

Traps

(see paragraph 1.4)

A.4 Minimum trap sizes and seal depths for appliances not listed in Table A2 are shown in Table A3.

Table A3 Minimum trap sizes and seal depths additional to Table 2

Appliance	Diam. of trap (mm)	Depth of seal (mm)
Sanitary towel macerator	40	75
Food waste disposal unit (industrial type)	50	75
Urinal stall (1 to 6 person position)	65	50

Branch discharge pipes

(see paragraph 1.10)

A.5 A branch pipe should not discharge into a stack less than 750mm above the invert of the tail of the bend at the foot of the stack in a multi-storey building up to 5 storeys. Alternatively a branch pipe serving any ground floor appliance may discharge direct to a drain or into its own stack.

A.6 If the building has more than 5 storeys ground floor appliances, unless discharging to a gully or drain, should discharge into their own stack. If the building has more than 20 storeys ground floor appliances, unless discharging to a gully or drain, and first floor appliances should discharge into their own stack.

Ventilating stacks

(see paragraph 1.21)

A.7 A dry stack may provide ventilation for branch ventilation pipes as an alternative to carrying them to outside air or to a ventilated discharge stack (ventilated system).

A.8 Ventilation stacks serving buildings with not more than 10 storeys and containing only dwellings should be at least 32mm diameter (for all other buildings see paragraph 1.29).

A.9 The lower end of a stack may be connected directly to a ventilated discharge stack below the lowest branch discharge pipe connection and above the bend at the foot of the stack or to the crown of the lowest branch discharge pipe connection providing it is ≥75mm diameter.

Greywater recovery systems

A.10 Sanitary pipework and underground drainage used to collect greywater for recovery and re-use within the building should be designed and constructed in accordance with the guidance in this Approved Document.

A.11 All pipework carrying greywater for re-use should be clearly marked with the word 'GREYWATER' in accordance with Water Regulations Advisory Scheme Information Guidance Note 09-02-05 *Marking and Identification of Pipework for Reclaimed and Grey Water Systems*.

A.12 Guidance on external storage tanks is given in Approved Document H2.

A.13 Further guidance on greywater recovery systems can be found in the Water Regulations Advisory Scheme leaflet No. 09-02-04 *Reclaimed Water Systems. Information about installing, modifying or maintaining reclaimed water systems*.

Appendix H1-B: Repairs, alterations and discontinued use of drains and sewers

Legislation

B.1   Although the Building Regulations do not include requirements for the continuing maintenance or repair of drains and sewers, local authorities and sewerage undertakers have powers to ensure that adequate maintenance is carried out, that repairs and alterations are carried out properly, and that disused drains and sewers are sealed.

Power to examine and test

B.2   Under Section 48 (Power of local authority to examine and test drains etc. believed to be defective) of the Public Health Act 1936 the local authority may test any drain or sewer where it appears to them that they have reasonable grounds for believing that is in such a condition:

a. as to be prejudicial to health or a nuisance (for example it is harbouring rats); or

b. (for those drains or sewers indirectly connecting to a public sewer) is so defective that groundwater leaks into it.

B.3   Under Section 114 (Power to investigate defective drain or sewer) of the Water Industry Act 1991, sewerage undertakers may examine and test any drain or private sewer connecting with a public sewer, where it appears to them that they have reasonable grounds for believing that is in such a condition:

a. as to be injurious or likely to cause injury to health or be a nuisance; or

b. is so defective that subsoil water leaks into it.

Power to require repairs

B.4   Under Section 59 (Drainage of building) of the Building Act 1984 the local authority may require the owner of a building to carry out remedial works where a soil pipe, drain or private sewer is:

a. insufficient;

b. in such a condition as to be prejudicial to health or a nuisance; or

c. so defective that subsoil water leaks into it.

Power to repair drains or private sewers

B.5   Under Section 17 (Power to repair drains etc. and to remedy stopped up drains etc.) of the Public Health Act 1961, as amended, local authorities have powers to repair or remove blockages on drains or private sewers which are not sufficiently maintained or kept in good repair or are stopped up, provided the cost does not exceed £250. They must first give notice to the owner. The costs may be recovered from the owner or owners of the drain or sewer.

Repair, reconstruction or alterations to underground drains or sewers

B.6   Although repairs, reconstruction or minor alterations to drains or sewers are not normally covered under the Building Regulations, local authorities have other powers to control such works.

B.7   Material alterations to existing drains and sewers are, however, covered under the Building Regulations.

B.8   **Notice to be given before repairs or alterations are carried out.** Under Section 61 (Repair etc. of drain) of the Building Act 1984, any person intending to repair, reconstruct or alter a drain must, except in an emergency, give 24 hours notice to the local authority of their intention to carry out the works. Where the works are carried out in an emergency they shall not cover over the work without giving such notice. They must also give free access to the local authority to inspect the works.

B.9   The local authority may, if appropriate, use their powers under Section 48 of the 1936 Public Health Act (see paragraph B.2) to test the drain, or under Section 59 of the Building Act 1984 (see paragraph B.4) to require remedial works.

Sealing or removal of disused drains or sewers

B.10   Disused drains and sewers offer ideal harbourage to rats and frequently offer a route for them to move between sewers and the surface. They could also collapse causing subsidence.

B.11   Under Section 62 (Disconnection of drain) of the Building Act 1984, any person who carries out works which result in any part of a drain becoming permanently disused, they shall seal the drain at such points as the local authority may direct.

B.12   Section 82 (Notices about demolition) of the Building Act 1984 allows the local authority to require any person demolishing a building to remove or seal any sewer or drain to which the building was connected.

B.13   Under Section 59 (Drainage of building) of the Building Act 1984, the local authority can require the owner of a building to remove, or otherwise render innocuous, any disused drain or sewer which is prejudicial to health or a nuisance.

Guidance

B.14 Paragraphs B.15 to B.19 give guidance on the appropriate methods associated with the repair and alteration of drains and sewers, and the removal or sealing of disused drains and sewers.

Repairs and alterations

B.15 Repairs, reconstruction and alterations to existing drains and sewers should be carried out to the same standards as new drains and sewers (see Approved Document H1 Section 2).

B.16 Where new pipework is connected to existing pipework, particular consideration should be given to the following points.

a. Ensuring that the existing pipework is not damaged, for example by using proper cutting equipment.

b. Ensuring that the resulting joint is water tight, for example by using purpose made repair couplings.

c. Ensuring that differential settlement does not occur between the existing and new pipework, for example by proper bedding of the pipework.

Sealing disused drains

B.17 Disused drains or sewers provide ideal nesting sites for rats. In order to prevent this disused drains or sewers should be disconnected from the sewer system as near as possible to the point of connection. This should be done in a manner which does not damage any pipe which is still in use and ensures that the sewer system is water tight. This may be carried out, for example, by removing the pipe from a junction and placing a stopper in the branch of the junction fitting. Where the connection was to a public sewer the sewerage undertaker should be consulted.

B.18 Drains or sewers less than 1.5m deep which are in open ground should as far as is practicable be removed. Other pipes should be sealed at both ends and at any point of connection, and grout filled to ensure that rats cannot gain access.

B.19 Larger pipes (225mm and above) should be grout filled to prevent subsidence or damage to buildings or services in the event of collapse.

Appendix H1-C: Adoption of sewers and connection to public sewers

C.1 There are a number of different ways in which a sewer may become a public sewer. Drains serving only one curtilage cannot be adopted by the sewerage undertaker.

An agreement with the sewerage undertaker to adopt sewers on completion

C.2 Under Section 104 (Agreements to adopt sewer or sewage disposal works at future date) of the Water Industry Act 1991, a sewerage undertaker may enter into an agreement with a developer to adopt a sewer at some time in the future subject to certain conditions. In cases of dispute appeals may be made to the Director General of Water Services.

C.3 Sewerage undertakers normally require the work to be carried out in accordance with their standards which are published in *Sewers for Adoption*.

Requisition of a sewer from the sewerage undertaker

C.4 Under Section 98 (Requisition of public sewer) of the Water Industry Act 1991, the owner or occupier of a building or proposed building or a local authority may requisition a sewer from the sewerage undertaker. The sewer is constructed by the sewerage undertaker who may use its rights of access to land. The person requisitioning the sewer may be required to contribute towards the cost of the sewer over a period of 12 years.

Adoption by the sewerage undertaker at the request of the owner

C.5 Under Section 102 (Adoption of sewers and disposal works) of the Water Industry Act 1991, a person may request a sewerage undertaker to adopt an existing sewer. The sewer should be in good condition and accessible. In cases of dispute, appeals may be made to the Director General of Water Services.

Adoption by the sewerage undertaker at its own volition

C.6 Under Section 102 (Adoption of sewers and disposal works) of the Water Industry Act 1991, a sewerage undertaker may decide to adopt an existing sewer of its own volition. The sewer should be in good condition and accessible. In cases of dispute, appeals may be made to the Director General of Water Services.

Making connections to public sewers

C.7 Under Section 106 (Right to communicate with public sewer) of the Water Industry Act 1991, the owner or occupier of a building has a right to connect to a public sewer subject to the following restrictions.

a. Where the public sewer is designated as either a foul sewer or a surface water sewer, the right is limited to connection of foul drains or surface water drains as appropriate.

b. The manner of the connection would not be prejudicial to the public sewer system.

c. 21 days notice is given to the sewerage undertaker of the intention to make the connection.

C.8 Under Section 107 (Right of undertaker to undertake making of communication with public sewers) of the Water Industry Act 1991, the sewerage undertaker may undertake the work of making the connection and recover their reasonable costs. Alternatively they may allow the developer to undertake to carry out the work under their supervision.

C.9 Guidance on making connections to existing sewers is given in paragraphs 2.15 and 2.16.

Drains which could be used to drain other developments

C.10 Section 112 of the Water Industry Act 1991 enables the sewerage undertaker to require that a drain or sewer be constructed in a different manner so that it may form part of the general system of drainage. The sewerage undertaker repays the person constructing the drain or sewer the additional costs of complying with the undertaker's requirement.

Where land or property neighbouring the applicant's site is likely to be developed, it would be prudent for the applicant to discuss the possibilities with the planning authority and the sewerage undertaker.

Adoption of surface water sewers by the Highway Authority

C.11 Under Section 37 (Highway created by dedication may become maintainable at public expense) or Section 38 (Power of highway authorities to adopt by agreement) of the Highways Act 1980, a highway authority may adopt, or agree to adopt in the future the drainage associated with a highway. Under Section 115 (Use of highway drains as sewers and vice versa) of the Water Industry Act 1991, the highway authority may agree that a highway drain may be used to drain rainwater from buildings. This power is descretionary.

Table C1 **Characteristics that should be considered when designing or laying a shared drain/sewer so that it meets the basic requirements for adoption**

a. Sewers should be designed and constructed in accordance with the Protocol on Design Construction and Adoption of Sewers in England and Wales	Protocol on Design, Construction and Adoption of Sewers in England and Wales, Defra, 2002
b. Sewers should be laid at an appropriate distance from buildings so as to avoid damage to the foundations	H1-2.17, H1-2.25 and Diagram 8. The distance from foundation to any drain is set out in H1-2.25. When building over a sewer the recommended minimum distance is 3m (H4-1.6)
c. The manholes and chambers, especially in private land, should be located so that they are, and continue to be, easily accessible manually or, if necessary, with maintenance equipment such as pipe jetters or mini-excavators. This is of particular importance where the depth would justify mechanical excavation to undertake repair work Although design codes indicate that access points may be up to 200m apart, it is unlikely that it would be possible to rod or safely pressure jet small-diameter pipes over such a distance; 100m is more appropriate	H1-2.51. Consult sewerage undertaker about access for plant
d. The last access point on the house drain should be sized to allow man entry and should be located in an accessible position. This access point should, as far as practicable, be located adjacent to the curtilage and preferably form an interface with the connection to the lateral where it runs outside the curtilage of the property to discharge into a sewer in a highway, into public open space or into third-party land As this final manhole is likely to be in position where vehicle or plant loading is anticipated, its construction should accord with Sewers for Adoption	H1-2.51
e. House 'collector' drains serving each property should normally discharge into the sewer via a single junction or a manhole	H1-2.13 to 2.16
f. Sewers should not be laid deeper than necessary, but in all cases the structural integrity of the pipe needs to be maintained. This can normally be done by providing a cover to the top of the pipe barrel of 1.2m or 0.9m in highways or private land respectively. If these depths are not practicable, special protection measures such as a concrete slab should be provided	H1-2.27 and BS EN 1295-1
g. Sizing and design of manholes and chambers should depend on the depth and on whether man entry is required. Manholes on or near highways or other roads need to be of robust construction	H1-2.48
h. Sewers should be laid in straight lines in both vertical and horizontal alignments	H1-2.19
j. The first preference should be to provide separate foul and surface water sewerage systems. Where 'combined' or 'partially combined' sewerage is unavoidable, the sizing and the design of that sewer should be enhanced in accordance with the current codes and design methodologies to make additional provisions to deal with the runoff	Requirement H5, H1-2.35 and H3-3.5. See also BS EN 752 Parts 3 and 4, particularly note Annex ND in BS EN 752 Part 4

The Requirement

This Approved Document, which took effect on 1 April 2002, deals with the following Requirement which is contained in the Building Regulations 2010.

Requirement	Limits on application
Wastewater treatment systems and cesspools **H2.** (1) Any septic tank and its form of secondary treatment, other wastewater treatment system or cesspool shall be so sited and constructed that: (a) it is not prejudicial to the health of any person; (b) it will not contaminate any watercourse, underground water or water supply; (c) there are adequate means of access for emptying and maintenance; and (d) where relevant, it will function to a sufficient standard for the protection of health in the event of a power failure. (2) Any septic tank, holding tank which is part of a wastewater treatment system or cesspool shall be: (a) of adequate capacity; (b) so constructed that it is impermeable to liquids; and (c) adequately ventilated. (3) Where a foul water drainage system from a building discharges to a septic tank, wastewater treatment system or cesspool, a durable notice shall be affixed in a suitable place in the building containing information on any continuing maintenance required to avoid risks to health.	

Guidance

Performance

In the Secretary of State's view the requirements of H2 will be met if:

a. wastewater treatment systems:

  i. have sufficient capacity to enable breakdown and settlement of solid matter in the wastewater from the buildings;

  ii. are sited and constructed so as to prevent overloading of the receiving water.

b. cesspools have sufficient capacity to store the foul water from the building until they are emptied;

c. wastewater treatment systems and cesspools are sited and constructed so as not to:

  i. be prejudicial to health or a nuisance;

  ii. adversely affect water sources or resources;

  iii. pollute controlled waters;

  iv. be in an area where there is a risk of flooding.

d. septic tanks and wastewater treatment systems and cesspools are constructed and sited so as to:

  i. have adequate ventilation;

  ii. prevent leakage of the contents and ingress of subsoil water.

e. having regard to water table levels at any time of the year and rising groundwater levels, drainage fields are sited and constructed so as to:

i. avoid overloading of the soakage capacity and

ii. provide adequately for the availability of an aerated layer in the soil at all times.

f. a notice giving information as to the nature and frequency of maintenance required for the cesspool or wastewater treatment system to continue to function satisfactorily is displayed within each of the buildings.

Introduction to provisions

0.1 A wastewater treatment system may be a septic tank, together with a drainage field or other means of secondary treatment, or other wastewater treatment system.

0.2 Paragraphs 1.1 to 1.72 give guidance only on the general principles relating to capacity, siting and ventilation of cesspools and wastewater treatment systems.

0.3 Any discharge from a wastewater treatment system is likely to require a consent from the Environment Agency.

Note: Initial contact with the Environment Agency is normally made as part of the planning procedures for non-mains drainage. Where there have not previously been such discussions with the Environment Agency, those seeking Building Regulations approval for non-mains drainage should contact the area office of the Environment Agency in order to determine whether a consent to discharge is required and what parameters apply. This should be done before an application is made for Building Regulations approval as it may have a direct bearing on the type of system that may be installed. Further information is available in the Environment Agency's Pollution Prevention Guideline No. 4 *Disposal of sewage where no mains drainage is available*.

0.4 Specialist knowledge is advisable in the detailed design and installation of small sewage treatment works and guidance is given in BS 6297:1983 *Code of practice for design and installation of small sewage treatment works and cesspools* (see also paragraph 1.72).

Options

1.1 The use of non-mains foul drainage, such as wastewater treatment systems or cesspools, should only be considered where connection to mains drainage is not practicable (see Approved Document H1).

1.2 **Septic tanks** provide suitable conditions for the settlement, storage and partial decomposition of solids which need to be removed at regular intervals. The discharge can, however, still be harmful and will require further treatment from either a drainage field/mound or constructed wetland.

1.3 Septic tanks with some form of secondary treatment will normally be the most economic means of treating wastewater from small developments (e.g. 1 to 3 dwellings). Appropriate forms of secondary treatment for use with septic tanks (drainage fields, drainage mounds or constructed wetlands) are described in paragraphs 1.4 to 1.10 below.

1.4 Drainage fields typically consist of a system of sub-surface irrigation pipes which allow the effluent to percolate into the surrounding soil. Biological treatment takes place naturally in the aerated layers of soil.

1.5 Drainage fields may be used to provide secondary treatment in conjunction with septic tanks. They may be used where the subsoil is sufficiently free-draining and the site is not prone to flooding or waterlogging at any time of year.

1.6 The Environment Agency does not permit drainage fields or drainage mounds in prescribed Zone 1 groundwater source-protection zones.

1.7 Drainage mounds are essentially drainage fields placed above the natural surface of the ground providing an aerated layer of soil to treat the discharge.

1.8 Drainage mounds may be used where the subsoil is occasionally waterlogged, but where drainage fields would otherwise be suitable.

1.9 Constructed wetlands (for example reed beds) are man-made systems which exploit the natural treatment capacity of certain wetland plants.

1.10 Constructed wetlands discharging to a suitable watercourse may be used to treat septic tank effluent where drainage fields are not practical. The consent of the Environment Agency may be required.

1.11 **Packaged treatment works** – This term is applied to a range of systems engineered to treat a given hydraulic and organic load using prefabricated components which can be installed with minimal site work. They use a number of processes which are different in detail, all treat effluent to a higher standard than septic tank systems and this normally allows direct discharge to a watercourse.

1.12 Packaged treatment works discharging to a suitable watercourse will normally be more economic for larger developments than septic tanks. They should also be considered where space is limited or where other options are not possible.

1.13 **Cesspools** – A cesspool is a watertight tank, installed underground, for the storage of sewage. No treatment is involved.

1.14 Where no other option is feasible a cesspool may be acceptable.

Septic tanks

1.15 Septic tanks should only be used in conjunction with a form of secondary treatment (e.g. a drainage field, drainage mound or constructed wetland).

Siting

1.16 Septic tanks should be sited at least 7m from any habitable parts of buildings, and preferably downslope.

1.17 Where they are to be emptied using a tanker, the septic tank should be sited within 30m of a vehicle access provided that the invert level of the septic tank is no more than 3m below the level of the vehicle access. This distance may need to be reduced where the depth to the invert of the tank is more than 3m. There should also be a clear route for the hose such that the tank can be emptied and cleaned without hazard to the building occupants and without the contents being taken through a dwelling or place of work.

Design and construction

1.18 Septic tanks should have a capacity below the level of the inlet of at least 2,700 litres (2.7m³) for up to 4 users. The size should be increased by 180 litres for each additional user.

1.19 Factory-made septic tanks are available in glass reinforced plastics, polyethylene or steel and should meet the requirements of BS EN 12566-1. Particular care is necessary in ensuring stability of these tanks.

1.20 Septic tanks may also be constructed in brickwork or concrete, roofed with heavy concrete slabs. Brickwork should be of engineering bricks and be at least 220mm thick. The mortar should be a mix of 1:3 cement–sand ratio. In situ concrete should be at least 150mm thick of C/25/P mix (see BS 5328).

1.21 Septic tanks should prevent leakage of the contents and ingress of subsoil water and should be ventilated. Ventilation should be kept away from buildings.

1.22 The inlet and outlet of a septic tank should be designed to prevent disturbance to the surface scum or settled sludge and should incorporate at least two chambers or compartments operating in series. Where the width of the tank does not exceed 1200mm the inlet should be via a dip pipe. To minimise turbulence, provision should be made to limit the flow rate of the incoming foul water. For steeply laid drains up to 150mm the velocity may be limited by laying the last 12m of the incoming drain at a gradient of 1 in 50 or flatter.

1.23 The inlet and outlet pipes of a septic tank should be provided with access for sampling and inspection (see Approved Document H1, paragraph 2.48).

1.24 Septic tanks should be provided with access for emptying and cleaning. Access covers should be of durable quality having regard to the corrosive nature of the tank contents. The access should be lockable or otherwise engineered to prevent personnel entry.

Marking

1.25 A notice should be fixed within the building describing the necessary maintenance. An example of such wording is:

'The foul drainage system from this property discharges to a septic tank and a <insert type of secondary treatment>. The tank requires monthly inspections of the outlet chamber or distribution box to observe that the effluent is free-flowing and clear. The septic tank requires emptying at least once every 12 months by a licensed contractor. The <insert type of secondary treatment> should be <insert details of maintenance of secondary treatment>. The owner is legally responsible to ensure that the system does not cause pollution, a health hazard or a nuisance.'

Drainage fields and drainage mounds

1.26 Paragraphs 1.27 to 1.44 give guidance on design and construction of drainage fields and drainage mounds to provide secondary treatment to the discharge from a septic tank or package treatment plant.

Siting

1.27 A drainage field or mound serving a wastewater treatment plant or septic tank should be located:

a. at least 10m from any watercourse or permeable drain;

b. at least 50m from the point of abstraction of any groundwater supply and not in any Zone 1 groundwater protection zone;

c. at least 15m from any building;

d. sufficiently far from any other drainage fields, drainage mounds or soakaways so that the overall soakage capacity of the ground is not exceeded.

1.28 The disposal area should be downslope of groundwater sources.

1.29 No water supply pipes or underground services other than those required by the disposal system itself should be located within the disposal area.

1.30 No access roads, driveways or paved areas should be located within the disposal area.

Ground conditions

1.31   Well drained and well aerated subsoils are usually brown, yellow or reddish in colour. Examples of subsoils with good percolation characteristics are sand, gravel, chalk, sandy loam and clay loam. It is important that the percolation characteristics are suitable in both summer and winter conditions. Poorly drained or saturated subsoils are often grey or blue in colour. Brown and grey mottling usually indicates periodic saturation. Examples of subsoils with poor percolation characteristics are sandy clay, silty clay and clay.

1.32   A preliminary assessment should be carried out including consultation with the Environment Agency and local authority to determine the suitability of the site. The natural vegetation on the site should also give an indication of its suitability for a drainage field.

1.33   A trial hole should be dug to determine the position of the standing groundwater table. The trial hole should be a minimum of 1m² in area and 2m deep, or a minimum of 1.5m below the invert of the proposed drainage field pipework. The groundwater table should not rise to within 1m of the invert level of the proposed effluent distribution pipes. If the test is carried out in summer, the likely winter groundwater levels should be considered. A percolation test should then be carried out to assess the further suitability of the proposed area.

1.34   **Percolation test method** – A hole 300mm square should be excavated to a depth 300mm below the proposed invert level of the effluent distribution pipe. Where deep drains are necessary the hole should conform to this shape at the bottom, but may be enlarged above the 300mm level to enable safe excavation to be carried out. Where deep excavations are necessary a modified test procedure may be adopted using a 300mm earth auger. Bore the test hole vertically to the appropriate depth taking care to remove all loose debris.

1.35   Fill the 300mm square section of the hole to a depth of at least 300mm with water and allow it to seep away overnight.

1.36   Next day, refill the test section with water to a depth of at least 300mm and observe the time, in seconds, for the water to seep away from 75% full to 25% full level (i.e. a depth of 150mm). Divide this time by 150. The answer gives the average time in seconds (V_p) required for the water to drop 1mm.

1.37   The test should be carried out at least three times with at least two trial holes. The average figure from the tests should be taken. The test should not be carried out during abnormal weather conditions such as heavy rain, severe frost or drought.

1.38   Drainage field disposal should only be used when percolation tests indicate average values of V_p of between 12 and 100 and the preliminary site assessment report and trial hole tests have been favourable. This minimum value ensures that untreated effluent cannot percolate too rapidly into groundwater. Where V_p is outside these limits effective treatment is unlikely to take place in a drainage field. However, provided that an alternative form of secondary treatment is provided to treat the effluent from the septic tanks, it may still be possible to discharge the treated effluent to a soakaway.

Design and construction

1.39   Drainage fields or mounds (see Diagrams 1 and 2) should be designed and constructed to ensure aerobic contact between the liquid effluent and the subsoil.

1.40   Drainage fields should be constructed using perforated pipe, laid in trenches of a uniform gradient which should be not steeper than 1:200.

1.41   Pipes should be laid on a 300mm layer of clean shingle or broken stone graded between 20mm and 50mm.

Diagram 1   **Drainage field**

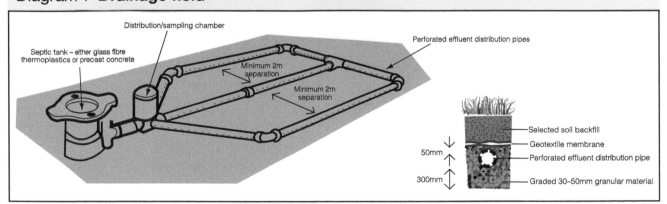

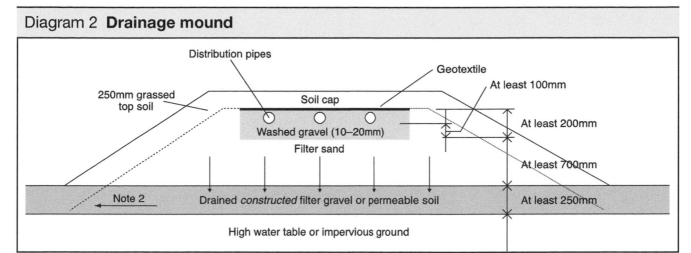

Diagram 2 **Drainage mound**

Distribution pipes

Geotextile

At least 100mm

250mm grassed top soil

Soil cap

At least 200mm

Washed gravel (10–20mm)

Filter sand

At least 700mm

Note 2

Drained *constructed* filter gravel or permeable soil

At least 250mm

High water table or impervious ground

Notes:

1. To provide venting of the filter, the upstream ends of the distribution pipes may be extended vertically above mound level and capped with a cowl or grille.

2. Surface water runoff and uncontaminated seepage from the surrounding soil may be cut off by shallow interceptor drains and diverted away from the mound. There must be no seepage of wastewater to such an interceptor drain.

3. Where the permeable soil is slow draining and overlaid on an impervious layer, the mound filter system should be constructed on a gently sloping site.

1.42 Trenches should be filled to a level 50mm above the pipe and covered with a layer of geotextile to prevent the entry of silt. The remainder of the trench can be filled with soil; the distribution pipes should be laid at a minimum depth of 500mm below the surface.

Drainage trenches should be from 300mm to 900mm wide, with areas of undisturbed ground 2m wide being maintained between parallel trenches (see Diagram 1).

1.43 An inspection chamber should be installed between the septic tank and the drainage field.

1.44 Drainage fields should be set out as a continuous loop fed from the inspection chamber (see Diagram 1). To calculate the floor area of the drainage field (A_t in m²), the following formula should be used:

$$A_t = p \times V_p \times 0.25$$

where p is the number of persons served by the tank, V_p is the percolation value (secs/mm) obtained as described in paragraphs 1.34–1.38.

Constructed wetlands/reed beds

1.45 Reed bed treatment systems or other constructed wetland treatment systems can be used to provide secondary or tertiary treatment of effluent from septic tanks or packaged treatment works. The systems purify wastewater as it moves through the gravel bed around the rhizomes and roots, by removing organic matter (BOD), oxidising ammonia, reducing nitrate and removing a little phosphorus. The mechanisms are complex and involve bacterial oxidation, filtration, sedimentation and chemical precipitation.

1.46 Reed beds generally use the common reed (*Phragmites australis*); other types of plants used in constructed wetlands include the reed maces (*Typha latifolia*), the rush (*Juncus effusus*),

the true bulrush (*Schoenoplectus lacustris*) as well as members of the sedge family (*Carex*) and the yellow flag (*Iris pseudacorus*).

1.47 Constructed wetlands should not be constructed in the shade of trees or buildings as this will result in poor or patchy growth. Although winter performance is generally similar with respect to removal of BOD and suspended solids, it tends to be poorer than in summer for removal of ammonia due to lower temperatures. This should be taken into consideration during the design stage.

1.48 There are two main designs of constructed wetland system, horizontal flow and vertical flow.

1.49 **Horizontal flow systems** are continuously fed with wastewater from one end. The effluent flows horizontally through the gravel bed over the full width of the bed to the outlet end (see Diagram 3). Horizontal flow systems tend to be oxygen limited and they therefore tend not to be able to completely treat concentrated effluents, particularly those with high levels of ammonia. Horizontal flow systems require a level site. As they only use a single bed less maintenance is required than with vertical flow systems.

1.50 **Vertical flow systems** are intermittently fed with wastewater from the top flooding the surface followed by a period of rest. For this reason two or more beds are normally provided so that they can be used in rotation. The flow is predominantly downward to an outlet at the bottom (see Diagram 4) and is collected by a drainage network at the base. They therefore require a fall of between 1m and 2m. Vertical flow systems can achieve much better oxygen transfer than horizontal flow systems and therefore achieve more complete treatment, particularly of ammonia. They generally require more maintenance than horizontal systems.

Diagram 3 Typical horizontal flow reed bed treatment system

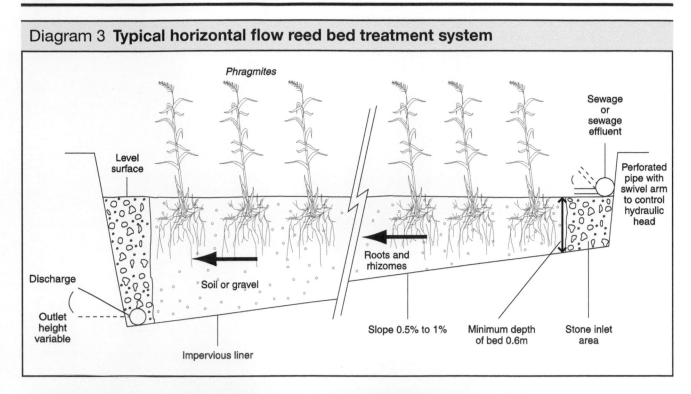

Phragmites

Level surface

Sewage or sewage effluent

Perforated pipe with swivel arm to control hydraulic head

Discharge

Outlet height variable

Roots and rhizomes

Soil or gravel

Impervious liner

Slope 0.5% to 1%

Minimum depth of bed 0.6m

Stone inlet area

Diagram 4 Typical vertical flow reed bed treatment system

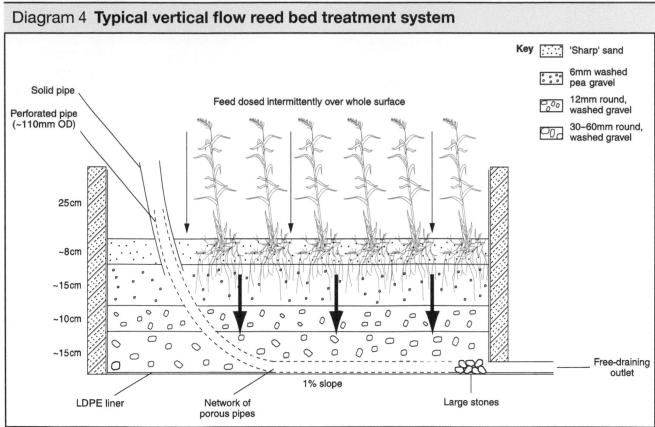

Key
- 'Sharp' sand
- 6mm washed pea gravel
- 12mm round, washed gravel
- 30–60mm round, washed gravel

Solid pipe

Perforated pipe (~110mm OD)

Feed dosed intermittently over whole surface

25cm

~8cm

~15cm

~10cm

~15cm

LDPE liner

Network of porous pipes

1% slope

Large stones

Free-draining outlet

1.51 Reed bed treatment systems should be designed and constructed in accordance with BRE Good Building Guide No. 42. Other forms of constructed wetland treatment system should be designed and constructed by specialists.

Marking

1.52 A notice should be fixed within the building describing the necessary maintenance. An example of such wording is:

'The foul drainage system from this building discharges to a *<insert type of primary treatment>* and a constructed wetland. The *<insert type of primary treatment>* requires *<insert details of maintenance of the primary treatment>*. The constructed wetland system requires *<insert details of maintenance of the constructed wetland>*.'

1.53 Guidance on maintenance requirements for reed bed treatment systems is given in BRE Good Building Guide No. 42.

Packaged treatment works

Siting

1.54 The discharge from the wastewater treatment plant should be sited at least 10m away from watercourses and any other buildings.

Design and construction

1.55 Packaged treatment works should be type-tested in accordance with BS 7781 or otherwise tested by a notified body.

1.56 If the packaged treatment works requires power to operate it should be able to adequately function without power for up to 6 hours or have an uninterruptable power supply.

Marking

1.57 A notice should be fixed within the building describing the necessary maintenance. An example of such wording is:

'The foul drainage system from this property discharges to a packaged treatment works. Maintenance is required *<insert frequency>* and should be carried out by the owner in accordance with the manufacturer's instructions. The owner is legally responsible to ensure that the system does not cause pollution, a health hazard or a nuisance.'

Cesspools

Siting

1.58 The site of the cesspool should preferably be on ground sloping away from and sited lower than any existing building in the immediate vicinity.

1.59 Cesspools should be sited at least 7m from any habitable parts of buildings and preferably downslope.

1.60 Cesspools should be sited within 30m of a vehicle access and at such levels that they can be emptied and cleaned without hazard to the building occupants or the contents being taken through a dwelling or place of work. Access may be through a covered space which may be lockable.

Design and construction

1.61 Cesspools should have a capacity below the level of the inlet of at least 18,000 litres (18m³) for 2 users. This size should be increased by 6800 litres (6.8m³) for each additional user.

1.62 Cesspools should have no openings except for the inlet, access for emptying and ventilation.

1.63 Cesspools should prevent leakage of the contents and ingress of subsoil water and should be ventilated.

1.64 Cesspools should be provided with access for emptying and cleaning. Access covers should be of durable quality having regard to the corrosive nature of the tank contents. The access should be lockable or otherwise engineered to prevent personnel entry.

1.65 Factory-made cesspools are available in glass reinforced plastics, polyethylene or steel and should meet the relevant requirements of BS EN 12566-1. Particular care is necessary in ensuring stability of these tanks.

1.66 Cesspools may be constructed in brickwork or concrete, roofed with heavy concrete slabs. Brickwork should be of engineering bricks and be at least 220mm thick. The mortar should be a mix of 1:3 cement–sand ratio. In situ concrete should be at least 150mm thick of C/25/P mix (see BS 5328).

1.67 The inlet of a cesspool should be provided with access for inspection (see Approved Document H1 Section 2).

Marking

1.68 A notice should be fixed within the building describing the necessary maintenance. An example of such wording is:

'The foul drainage system from this property is served by a cesspool. The system should be emptied approximately every *<insert design emptying frequency>* by a licensed contractor and inspected fortnightly for overflow. The owner is legally responsible to ensure that the system does not cause pollution, a health hazard or a nuisance.'

Greywater and rainwater storage tanks

1.69   Paragraphs 1.70 to 1.71 give guidance on tanks for the storage of greywater or rainwater for re-use within the building. It does not apply to water butts used for the storage of rainwater for garden use.

1.70   Greywater and rainwater tanks should:

a. prevent leakage of the contents and ingress of subsoil water, and should be ventilated;

b. have an anti-backflow device on any overflow connected to a drain or sewer to prevent contamination of the stored greywater or rainwater in the event of surcharge in the drain or sewer;

c. be provided with access for emptying and cleaning. Access covers should be of durable quality having regard to the corrosive nature of the tank contents. The access should be lockable or otherwise engineered to prevent personnel entry.

1.71   Further guidance on systems for greywater and rainwater re-use can be found in the Water Regulations Advisory Scheme leaflet No. 09-02-04. *Reclaimed Water Systems. Information about installing, modifying or maintaining reclaimed water systems.*

Alternative approach

1.72   The requirement can also be met by following the relevant recommendations of BS 6297:1983 *Code of practice for design and installation of small sewage treatment works and cesspools.* The relevant clauses are in Section 1, Section 2, Section 3 (Clauses 6–11), Section 4 and Appendices.

Appendix H2-A: Maintenance of wastewater treatment systems and cesspools

Legislation

A.1   Local authorities have powers to ensure that wastewater treatment systems or cesspools are adequately maintained.

Power to examine and test

A.2   Under Section 48 (Power of local authority to examine and test drains etc. believed to be defective) of the Public Health Act 1936, the local authority may test any cesspool, septic tank or settlement tank where it appears to them that they have reasonable grounds for believing that it is in such a condition as to be prejudicial to health or a nuisance.

Power in respect of overflowing or leaking cesspools, septic tanks, etc.

A.3   Under Section 50 (Overflowing and leaking cesspools) of the Public Health Act 1936, the local authority can take action against any person who has caused by their action, default or sufferance, a septic tank, settlement tank or cesspool to leak or overflow. They may require the person to carry out repairs or to periodically empty the tank.

A.4   This does not apply to the overflow of treated effluent or flow from a septic tank into a drainage field, provided the overflow is not prejudicial to health or a nuisance.

A.5   It should be noted that under this section action could be taken against a builder who had caused the problem, and not just against the owner.

Power to require repairs

A.6   Under Section 59 (Drainage of building) of the Building Act 1984, the local authority may require the owner or occupier of a building to carry out remedial works where a septic tank, settlement tank or cesspool is:

a.   insufficient;

b.   in such a condition as to be prejudicial to health or a nuisance; or

c.   so defective that groundwater leaks into it.

Disused septic tanks, cesspools, etc.

A.7   Also under Section 59 (Drainage of building) of the Building Act 1984, where a disused cesspool, septic tank or settlement tank is prejudicial to health or a nuisance, the local authority may require either the owner or the occupier to fill or remove the tank or otherwise render it innocuous.

Powers of the Environment Agency

A.8   The Environment Agency has powers under Section 85 (Offences of polluting controlled waters) of the Water Resources Act 1991 to prosecute anyone causing or knowingly permitting pollution of any stream, river, lake, etc. or any groundwater.

A.9   They also have powers under Section 161A (Notices requiring persons to carry out anti-pollution works and operations) of the Water Resources Act 1991 (as amended by the Environment Act 1995) to take action against any person causing or knowingly permitting a situation in which pollution of a stream, river, lake, etc. or groundwater is likely. They can require such a person to carry out works to prevent the pollution.

GUIDANCE ON MAINTENANCE

A.10   Paragraphs A.11 to A.22 give guidance on the appropriate maintenance of wastewater treatment systems and cesspools.

Septic tanks

A.11   Septic tanks should be inspected monthly to check they are working correctly. The effluent in the outlet from the tank should be free-flowing and clear. The flow in the inlet chamber should also be free-flowing.

A.12   If the flow is incorrect, the tank should be emptied by a licensed contractor. Some contractors offer annual maintenance contracts at reduced rates.

A.13   The septic tank should be emptied at least once a year. It is recommended that not all sludge is removed as it can act as an anaerobic seed.

A.14   If the tank is not adequately maintained and solids are carried into a drainage field/mound, the sediments can block the pores in the soil, necessitating the early replacement of the drainage field/mound. Occasionally, it can render the site unsuitable for future use as drainage field/mound.

Drainage fields and mounds

A.15   The drainage field/mound should be checked on a monthly basis to ensure that it is not waterlogged and that the effluent is not backing up towards the septic tank.

Packaged treatment works

A.16   The outlet of the works should be inspected regularly. The effluent should be free-flowing and clear.

A.17 Maintenance will vary depending on the type of plant; regular maintenance and inspection should be carried out in accordance with the manufacturer's instructions.

A.18 Where the treatment works serve more than one property, the developer may seek to get it adopted by the sewerage undertaker under Section 102 (Adoption of sewers and disposal works) or Section 104 (Agreements to adopt a sewer or disposal works at a future date) of the Water Industry Act 1991 (see Approved Document H1, Appendix H1-B).

Constructed wetlands/reed beds

A.19 Guidance on maintenance of reed beds can be found in BRE Good Building Guide No. 42.

Cesspools

A.20 Cesspools should be inspected fortnightly for overflow and emptied as required.

A.21 Typically they require emptying on a monthly basis by a licensed contractor.

A.22 Emptying frequencies may be estimated by assuming a filling rate of 150 litres per person per day. If the cesspool does not fill within the estimated period, the tank should be checked for leakage.

The Requirement

This Approved Document, which took effect on 1 April 2002, deals with the following Requirement which is contained in the Building Regulations 2010.

Requirement	Limits on application
Rainwater drainage	
H3. (1) Adequate provision shall be made for rainwater to be carried from the roof of the building.	
(2) Paved areas around the building shall be so constructed as to be adequately drained.	Requirement H3(2) applies only to paved areas:
	(a) which provide access to the building pursuant to requirement M1 (access and use of buildings other than dwellings), or requirement M2 (access to extensions to buildings other than dwellings), or requirement M4(1), (2) or (3) (access to and use of dwellings);
	(b) which provide access to or from a place of storage pursuant to requirement H6(2) (solid waste storage); or
	(c) in any passage giving access to the building, where this is intended to be used in common by the occupiers of one or more other buildings.
(3) Rainwater from a system provided pursuant to sub-paragraphs (1) or (2) shall discharge to one of the following, listed in order of priority:	Requirement H3(3) does not apply to the gathering of rainwater for re-use.
(a) an adequate soakaway or some other adequate infiltration system; or, where that is not reasonably practicable,	
(b) a watercourse; or, where that is not reasonably practicable,	
(c) a sewer.	

Guidance

Performance

In the Secretary of State's view the requirements of H3 will be met if:

a. rainwater from roofs and paved areas is carried away from the surface either by a drainage system or by other means;

b. a rainwater drainage system:

  i. carries the flow of rainwater from the roof to an outfall (a soakaway, a watercourse, a surface water or a combined sewer),

  ii. minimises the risk of blockage or leakage,

  iii. is accessible for clearing blockages.

c. rainwater soaking into the ground is distributed sufficiently so that it does not damage the foundations of the proposed building or any adjacent structure.

Introduction to provisions

0.1 The provisions in this document in relation to the drainage of paved areas apply only to paved areas:

a. within the curtilage of a building which are

   i. provided in accordance with requirements M2 and M4, to provide access to the principal entrance (see Approved Document M volume 2 section 1 for buildings other than dwellings and Approved Document M volume 1 sections 1A, 2A and 3A for dwellings);

   ii. provided in accordance with requirement H6 to give access from the building to the place for storing refuse, and from the place of storage to the collection point (see Approved Document H6);

b. which are yards or other forms of access intended to be used in common by more than one building.

The provisions of H3 only apply if these surfaces are paved.

0.2 Methods of drainage other than connection to a public surface water sewer are encouraged where they are technically feasible.

0.3 The capacity of the drainage system should be large enough to carry the expected flow at any point in the system.

0.4 The flow depends on the area to be drained and the intensity of the rainfall.

0.5 The capacity depends on the size and gradient of the gutters and pipes. Capacities and minimum sizes are given in the text.

0.6 Rainwater or surface water should not be discharged to a cesspool or septic tank.

Section 1: Gutters and rainwater pipes

Design rainfall intensities

1.1 For eaves, gutters the rainfall intensity should be obtained from Diagram 1.

1.2 Where the design incorporates valley gutters, parapet gutters, siphonic or drainage systems from flat roofs, and where over-topping of these systems would have particularly high consequences such as water entering the building, wetting of insulation or other dampness the design should be carried out in accordance with BS EN 12056 (see paragraph 1.17).

Gutters

1.3 The flow into a gutter depends on the area of surface being drained and whether the surface is flat or pitched (and, if it is pitched, on the angle of pitch). Table 1 shows a way of allowing for the pitch by working out an effective area.

1.4 Table 2 shows the largest effective area which should be drained into the gutter sizes which are most often used. These sizes are for a gutter which is laid level, half round in section with a sharp edged outlet at only one end and where the distance from a stop end to the outlet is not more than 50 times the water depth. At greater distances the capacity of the gutter should be reduced. The Table shows the smallest size of outlet which should be used with the gutter.

1.5 Where the outlet is not at the end, the gutter should be of the size appropriate to the larger of the areas draining into it. Where there are two end outlets they may be up to 100 times the depth of flow apart.

Table 1 Calculation of drained area

	Type of surface	Effective design area
1	Flat roof	plan area of relevant portion
2	Pitched roof at 30° Pitched roof at 45° Pitched roof at 60°	plan area of portion x 1.29 plan area of portion x 1.50 plan area of portion x 1.87
3	Pitched roof over 70° or any wall	elevational area x 0.5

Table 2 Gutter sizes and outlet sizes

Max. effective roof area (m²)	Gutter size (mm diam.)	Outlet size (mm diam.)	Flow capacity (litres/sec)
6.0	–	–	–
18.0	75	50	0.38
37.0	100	63	0.78
53.0	115	63	1.11
65.0	125	75	1.37
103.0	150	89	2.16

Note: Refers to nominal half round eaves gutters laid level with outlets at one end sharp edged. Round edged outlets allow smaller downpipe sizes.

Diagram 1 Rainfall intensities for design of gutter and rainfall pipes (litres per second per square metre)

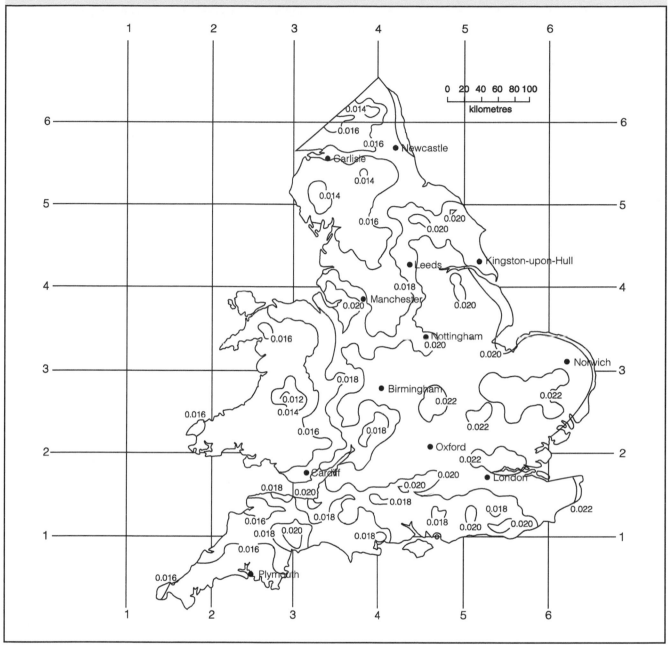

Rainwater pipes

1.6 Gutters should be laid with any fall towards the nearest outlet. Where there is a fall or the gutter has a section which gives it larger capacity than a half-round gutter or the outlet is round edged it may be possible to reduce the size of the gutter and pipe.

Paragraph 1.17 gives a reference to some detailed recommendations which make reductions possible.

1.7 Gutters should also be laid so that any overflow in excess of the design capacity, caused by conditions such as above normal rainfall, will be discharged clear of the building, reducing the risk of overspilling of rainwater into the building or structural overload. On flat roofs, valley gutter, and parapet gutters, additional outlets may be necessary.

1.8 Rainwater pipes should discharge into a drain or gully but may discharge to another gutter or onto another surface if it is drained. Any rainwater pipe which discharges into a combined system should do so through a trap (see Approved Document H1).

1.9 Where a rainwater pipe discharges onto a lower roof or paved area, a pipe shoe should be fitted to divert water away from the building. Where rainwater from a roof with an effective area greater than 25m² discharges through a single downpipe onto a lower roof, a distributor pipe should be fitted to the shoe to ensure that the flow width at the receiving gutter is sufficient so that it does not over-top the gutter.

1.10 The size of a rainwater pipe should be at least the size of the outlet from the gutter. A down pipe which serves more than one gutter should have an area at least as large as the largest of the contributing outlets and should be of sufficient size to take the flow from the whole contributing area.

Siphonic roof drainage systems

1.11 Siphonic roof drainage systems should be designed in accordance with BS EN 12056-3 (see paragraph 1.17) and should take particular account of the following:

a. The need to take account of surcharge in the downstream drainage system as this can reduce the flow in the downpipe.

b. For long gutters the time taken for the system to prime the siphonic action may be excessive. Overflow arrangements should be provided to prevent gutters from over-topping.

1.12 Further information on the design of siphonic drainage systems can be found in Hydraulics Research Ltd Report SR 463 *Performance of Syphonic Drainage Systems for Roof Gutters*.

Eaves drop systems

1.13 Eaves drop systems allow rainwater from roofs to drop freely to the ground. Where these are used, they should be designed taking into account the following:

a. the protection of the fabric of the building from ingress of water, caused by water splashing on the external walls;

b. the need to prevent water from entering doorways and windows;

c. the need to protect persons using doorways, etc. from falling water;

d. the need to protect persons and the fabric of the building from rainwater as it hits the ground by splashing, for example by provision of a gravel layer or angled concrete apron deflecting the water away from the building;

e. the protection of foundations from concentrated discharges such as those from valleys or valley gutters or from excessive flows due to large roofs (i.e. where the area of roof per unit length of eaves is high).

Rainwater recovery systems

1.14 Rainwater drainage systems used to collect water for re-use within the building (rainwater recovery systems) should take account of the following:

a. storage tanks should comply with requirement H2 (see Approved Document H2 paragraphs 1.69 to 1.71);

b. pipework, washouts and valves should be clearly identified on marker plates (see Water Regulations Advisory Scheme Information Guidance Note 09-02-05 *Marking and Identification of Pipework for Reclaimed and Grey Water Systems*).

1.15 Further guidance on rainwater recovery systems can be found in the Water Regulations Advisory Scheme leaflet No. 09-02-04. *Reclaimed Water Systems. Information about installing, modifying or maintaining reclaimed water systems*.

Materials for gutters, rainwater pipes and joints

1.16 The materials used should be of adequate strength and durability, and

a. all gutter joints should remain water tight under working conditions. Pipes inside a building should be capable of withstanding the air tightness test described in paragraph 1.32 of Approved Document H1, and

b. pipework in siphonic roof drainage systems should be able to resist to negative pressures in accordance with the design, and

c. gutters and rainwater pipes should be firmly supported without restricting thermal movement, and

d. different metals should be separated by non-metallic material to prevent electrolytic corrosion.

Alternative approach

1.17 The performance can also be met by following the relevant recommendations of BS EN 12056 *Gravity drainage systems inside buildings*. The relevant clauses are in Part 3 *Roof drainage layout and calculation*, Clauses 3 to 7, annex A and National Annexes, and in Part 5 *Installation, testing instructions for operation maintenance and use*, Clauses 3, 4, 6 and 11. These standards contain additional detailed information about design and construction.

Section 2: Drainage of paved areas

2.1 This section gives guidance on the design of paved areas for rainwater drainage systems. It is applicable to the drainage of paved areas around buildings and small car parks up to 4,000m². For the design of systems serving larger catchments, reference should be made to BS EN 752-4 (see paragraph 2.19).

2.2 Surface gradients should direct water draining from a paved area away from buildings. Where the levels would otherwise cause water to concentrate along the wall of a building, a reverse gradient should be created, for at least 500mm from the wall of the building, to divert the water away from the wall.

Diagram 2 **Rainfall intensities for design of drainage from paved areas and underground rainwater drainage (litres per second per square metre)**

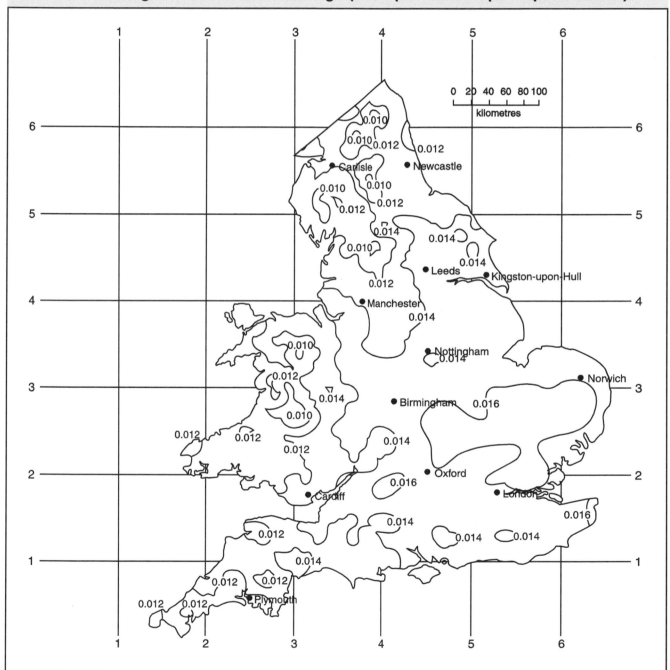

2.3   Gradients on impervious surfaces should be designed to permit the water to drain quickly from the surface. A gradient of at least 1 in 60 is recommended. The gradient across a path should not exceed 1 in 40.

Design rainfall intensities

2.4   Design rainfall intensities of 0.014 litres/second/m² may be assumed for normal situations. Where ponding of rainfall is undesirable rainfall intensities should be obtained from Diagram 2.

2.5   For very high risk areas, where ponding would lead to flooding of buildings, the drainage should be designed in accordance with BS EN 752-4 (see paragraph 2.19).

Freedraining surfaces

2.6   Paths, driveways and other narrow areas of paving should be freedraining to a pervious area such as grassland, provided that:

a. the water is not discharged adjacent to buildings where it could damage foundations; and

b. the soakage capacity of the ground is not overloaded.

2.7   Where water is to be drained onto the adjacent ground the edge of the paving should be finished above or flush with the surrounding ground to allow the water to runoff.

2.8   Where the surrounding ground is not sufficiently permeable to accept the flow, filter drains may be provided (see paragraph 3.33).

Pervious paving

2.9   Pervious paving consists of a porous or permeable surface overlying a granular layer which acts as a storage reservoir, retaining peak flows while the water soaks into the underlying subsoil. They should be considered for larger paved areas where it is not possible to drain the rainwater to an adjacent pervious area. The design of the storage layer is undertaken on a similar basis to the design of the storage volume in soakaways (see paragraphs 3.24–3.28). Where infiltration is not possible (see paragraph 3.25), they may also be used with an impermeable barrier below the storage layer as a detention tank prior to flows discharging to a drainage system (see paragraph 3.35).

2.10   For steeply sloping surfaces, a check should be made to ensure that the water level can rise sufficiently in the granular storage layer to allow the storage capacity to be mobilised. A check should also be made to ensure that the stored water will not accumulate around the foundations of the building. Where infiltration is not possible (see paragraph 3.25), they may also be used with an impermeable barrier below the storage layer as a detention tank prior to flows discharging to a drainage system (see paragraph 3.35).

2.11   Pervious paving should not be used where excessive amounts of sediment are likely to enter the pavement and block the pores.

2.12   Pervious paving should not be used in oil storage areas, or where runoff may be contaminated with pollutants. Surface water should not be allowed to soak into the ground where ground conditions are not suitable (see paragraph 3.25).

2.13   Further information on pervious paving can be obtained from CIRIA report C522 – *Sustainable urban drainage systems – design manual for England and Wales*.

Drainage systems

2.14   Where it is not possible for surfaces to be freedraining, or to use pervious paving, impervious paving should be used with gullies or channels discharging to a drainage system.

2.15   Gullies should be provided at low points where water would otherwise pond. Intermediate gullies should be provided at intervals to ensure that gullies are not overloaded and the depth of flow in channels is not excessive.

2.16   Gully gratings should be set approximately 5mm below the level of the surrounding paved area in order to allow for settlement.

2.17   Provision should be made to prevent silt and grit entering the system, either by provision of gully pots of suitable size or by catchpits.

2.18   Drainage from large paved areas should be designed in accordance with BS EN 752-4 (see 2.19).

Alternative approach

2.19   The performance can also be met by following the relevant recommendations of BS EN 752-4:1998 *Drain and sewer systems outside buildings,* Part 4 *Hydraulic design and environmental aspects*. The relevant clauses are

Clause 11 and National Annexes ND and NE.

Section 3: Surface water drainage

3.1 This section gives guidance on the design of surface water drainage systems. It is applicable to the drainage of small catchments with impervious areas up to 2 hectares. For the design of systems serving larger catchments, reference should be made to BS EN 752-4 (see paragraph 3.36).

Outlets

3.2 Surface water drainage should discharge to a soakaway or other infiltration system where practicable.

3.3 Discharge to a watercourse may require a consent from the Environment Agency, who may limit the rate of discharge. Maximum flow rates can be limited by provision of detention basins (see paragraph 3.35).

3.4 Where other forms of outlet are not practicable, discharge should be made to a sewer.

Combined systems

3.5 Some sewers carry both foul water and surface water (combined systems) in the same pipe. Where they do the sewerage undertaker can allow surface water to discharge into the system if the sewer has enough capacity to take the added flow (see Approved Document H1 paragraph 2.1). Some private sewers (drains serving more than one building that have not been adopted by the sewerage undertaker) also carry both foul water and surface water. If a sewer operated as a combined system does not have enough capacity, the surface water should be run in a separate system with its own outfall.

3.6 In some circumstances, where a sewer is operated as a combined system and has sufficient capacity, separate drainage should still be provided (see Approved Document H5).

3.7 Surface water drainage connected to combined sewers should have traps on all inlets.

Design rainfall intensities

3.8 Design rainfall intensities of 0.014 litres/second/m² may be assumed for normal situations. Alternatively the rainfall intensity may be obtained from Diagram 2.

3.9 Where low levels of surface flooding could cause flooding of buildings the rainfall intensities should be obtained from BS EN 752-4 (see paragraph 3.36).

Design

3.10 Where there is evidence of a liability to surcharging from sewers, or levels in the building or on the site make gravity connection impracticable, surface water lifting equipment will be needed (see Approved Document H1 paragraphs 2.8 to 2.12).

Layout

3.11 Refer to paragraphs 2.13 to 2.21 of Approved Document H1.

Depth of pipes

3.12 Refer to paragraphs 2.27 and 2.28 of Approved Document H1.

Pipe gradients and sizes

3.13 Drains should have enough capacity to carry the flow. The capacity depends on the size and gradients of the pipes.

3.14 Drains should be at least 75mm diameter. Surface water sewers (serving more than one building) should have a minimum size of 100mm. Diagram 3 shows the capacities of drains of various sizes at different gradients. However the capacity can be increased by increasing the gradient, or by using larger pipes.

3.15 75mm and 100mm rainwater drains should be laid at not less than 1:100. 150mm drains and sewers should be laid at gradients not less than 1:150 and 225mm drains should be laid at gradients not less than 1:225. For minimum gradients for larger pipes see BS EN 752-4 (see paragraph 3.36).

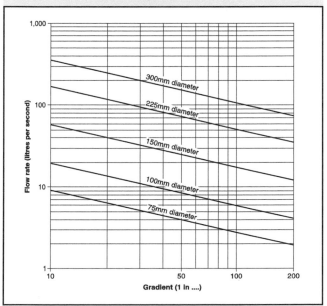

Diagram 3 **Discharge capacities of rainwater drains running full**

Materials for pipes and jointing

3.16 See paragraph 2.40 of Approved Document H1.

Bedding and backfilling

3.17 See paragraphs 2.41 to 2.45 of Approved Document H1.

Clearance of blockages

3.18 See paragraphs 2.46 to 2.54 of Approved Document H1.

Workmanship

3.19 See paragraphs 2.55 to 2.58 of Approved Document H1.

Testing and inspection

3.20 See paragraphs 2.59 to 2.62 of Approved Document H1.

Contaminated runoff

3.21 Where any materials which could cause pollution are stored or used, separate drainage systems should be provided. This should include an appropriate form of separator or treatment system or the flow should be discharged into a system suitable for receiving polluted effluent.

3.22 On car parks, petrol filling stations or other areas where there is likely to be leakage or spillage of oil, drainage systems should be provided with oil interceptors (see Appendix H3-A).

Soakaways and other infiltration drainage systems

3.23 Infiltration devices include soakaways, swales, infiltration basins and filter drains.

3.24 Further information on the design of infiltration drainage systems can be found in CIRIA Report 156 – *Infiltration drainage – Manual of good practice*.

3.25 Infiltration drainage is not always possible. Infiltration devices should not be built:

a. within 5m of a building or road or in areas of unstable land (see Planning Policy Guidance Note 14 Annex 1);

b. in ground where the water table reaches the bottom of the device at any time of the year;

c. sufficiently far from any drainage fields, drainage mounds or other soakaways so that the overall soakage capacity of the ground is not exceeded and the effectiveness of any drainage field is not impaired (see Approved Document H2);

d. where the presence of any contamination in the runoff could result in pollution of a groundwater source or resource.

3.26 **Soakaways** for areas less than 100m² are generally formed from square or circular pits, filled with rubble or lined with dry-jointed masonry or perforated ring units. Soakaways serving larger areas are generally lined pits or trench type soakaways.

3.27 Soakaways should be designed to a return period of once in ten years. The design should be carried out with storms of differing durations to determine the duration which gives the largest storage volume. For small soakaways serving 25m² or less a design rainfall of 10mm in 5 minutes may be assumed to give the worst case. For soakaways serving larger areas reference should be made to the sources listed in paragraph 3.30. Where the ground is marginal overflow drains can be acceptable.

3.28 Percolation tests should be carried out to determine the capacity of the soil (see Approved Document H2 paragraphs 1.34 to 1.38). Where the test is carried out in accordance with Approved Document H2, the soil infiltration rate (f) is related to the value Vp derived from the test by the equation:

$$f = \frac{10^{-3}}{3V_p}$$

3.29 The storage volume should be calculated so that, over the duration the storm, it is sufficient to contain the difference between the inflow volume and the outflow volume. The inflow volume is calculated from the rainfall depth (see paragraph 3.26) and the area drained. The outflow volume (O) is calculated from the equation:

$$O = a_{s50} \times f \times D$$

Where a_{s50} is the area of the side of the storage volume when filled to 50% of its effective depth, and D is the duration of the storm in minutes.

3.30 Soakaways serving larger areas should be designed in accordance with BS EN 752-4 (see paragraph 3.36), or BRE Digest *365 Soakaway design*.

Other types of infiltration system

3.31 **Swales** are grass-lined channels which transport rainwater from a site as well as controlling flow and quality of surface runoff. Some of the flow infiltrates into the ground. There may be an overflow at the end into another form of infiltration device or a watercourse. They are particularly suitable for treatment of runoff from small residential developments, parking areas and roads.

3.32 **Infiltration basins** are dry grass-lined basins designed to promote infiltration of surface water to the ground.

3.33 Filter drains or french drains consist of the trench, lined with a geotextile membrane and filled with gravel. Much of the flow infiltrates into the ground. A perforated pipe is often laid through the gravel to assist drainage.

3.34 Flow enters the top of the filter drain directly from runoff, or is discharged into it through drains.

Detention ponds

3.35 Detention ponds are used to attenuate the flow from a drainage system, to limit the peak rate of flow into a sewer system or watercourse. Further information on design may be found in the references given in paragraph 3.36 and in *Sustainable Urban Drainage Systems – A Design Manual for England and Wales* published by CIRIA.

Alternative approach

3.36 The requirement can also be met by following the relevant recommendations of BS EN 752-4 *Drain and sewer systems outside buildings*. The relevant clauses are in Part 4 *Hydraulic design and environmental considerations* Clauses 3 to 12 and National Annexes NA, NB and ND to NI. BS EN 752, together with BS EN 1295 and BS EN 1610, contains additional detailed information about design and construction.

Appendix H3-A: Oil separators

Legislation

A.1 Under Section 85 (Offences of polluting controlled waters) of the Water Resources Act 1991, it is an offence to discharge any noxious or polluting material into a watercourse, coastal water or underground water. Most surface water sewers discharge to watercourses.

A.2 Under Section 111 (Restrictions on use of public sewers) of the Water Industry Act 1991, it is an offence to discharge petrol into any drain or sewer connected to a public sewer.

A.3 Premises keeping petrol must be licensed under the Petroleum (Consolidation) Act 1928. Conditions may be placed on licences.

A.4 The Environment Agency issues guidance notes on the provision of oil separators.

A.5 The Health and Safety Executive issues guidance notes on the storage of oil.

Technical guidance

A.6 For most paved areas around buildings or car parks where a separator is required, a by-pass separator should be provided which has a nominal size (NSB) equal to 0.0018 times the contributing area. In addition it should have a silt storage volume in litres equal to 100 times NSB.

A.7 In fuel storage areas and other high risk areas full retention separators are required. These should have a nominal size (NS) equal to 0.018 times the contributing area. In addition it should have a silt storage volume in litres equal to 100 times NS.

A.8 Separators discharging to infiltration devices or surface water sewers should be Class I.

A.9 Separators should be leak tight. Inlet arrangements should not be direct to the water surface. Adequate ventilation should be provided.

A.10 Separators should comply with the requirements of the Environment Agency and with BS EN 858-2002 A1 2004 and BS EN 858-2:2003. In addition, where the Petroleum Act applies, they should comply with the requirements of the licensing authority.

A.11 Separators should be maintained regularly to ensure their continued effectiveness. Provision should be made for access for inspection and maintenance.

A.12 Further information on provision of separators is available in *Use and design of oil separators in surface drainage systems*, Pollution Prevention Guideline No. 3. This can be obtained from the Environment Agency.

The Requirement

This Approved Document, which took effect on 1 April 2002, deals with the following Requirement which is contained in the Building Regulations 2010.

Requirement	Limits on application
Building over sewers	Requirement H4 applies only to work carried out:
H4. (1) The erection or extension of a building or work involving the underpinning of a building shall be carried out in a way that is not detrimental to the building or building extension or to the continued maintenance of the drain, sewer or disposal main.	(a) over a drain, sewer or disposal main which is shown on any map of sewers; or
(2) In this paragraph 'disposal main' means any pipe, tunnel or conduit used for the conveyance of effluent to or from a sewage disposal works, which is not a public sewer.	(b) on any site or in such a manner as may result in interference with the use of, or obstruction of the access of any person to, any drain, sewer or disposal main which is shown on any map of sewers.
(3) In this paragraph and paragraph H5 'map of sewers' means any records kept by a sewerage undertaker under section 199 of the Water Industry Act 1991 (**a**).	

(**a**) 1991 c. 56; Section 199 was amended by Section 97 of the Water Act 2003 (c. 37).

Guidance

Performance

In the Secretary of State's view the requirements of H4 will be met if:

a. the building or extension or work involving underpinning:

   i. is constructed or carried out in a manner which will not overload or otherwise cause damage to the drain, sewer or disposal main either during or after the construction;

   ii. will not obstruct reasonable access to any manhole or inspection chamber on the drain, sewer or disposal main;

b. in the event of the drain, sewer or disposal main requiring replacement, there is a satisfactory diversionary route or the building or the extension will not unduly obstruct work to replace the drain, sewer or disposal main, on its present alignment;

c. the risk of damage to the building as a result of failure of the drain, sewer or disposal main is not excessive having regard to:

   i. the nature of the ground;

   ii. the condition, location or construction of the drain, sewer or disposal main;

   iii. the nature, volume and pressure of the flow in the drain, sewer or disposal main;

   iv. the design and construction of the foundations of the building.

Introduction to provisions

0.1   These provisions apply to the construction, extension or underpinning of a building over or within 3m of the centreline of an existing drain, sewer or disposal main shown on the sewerage undertaker's sewer records whether that sewer is a public sewer or not.

0.2   Copies of the sewer record maps are held by the sewerage undertaker and by local authorities. These are available for inspection during office hours.

0.3 Where it is proposed to construct a building over or near a drain or sewer shown on any map of sewers, the developer should consult the owner of the drain or sewer, if the owner is not the developer himself. In the case of a public sewer the owner is the sewerage undertaker, who may be able to advise on the condition of the sewer or arrange an inspection.

0.4 If repair or replacement of a public sewer is required it will be carried out by the sewerage undertaker.

0.5 Where it is proposed to construct a building or extension over a sewer which is intended for adoption, it is advisable to consult the sewerage undertaker.

Undue risk in the event of failure of the drain or sewer

1.1 Some soils are easily eroded by groundwater leaking into the drain or sewer. Examples of such soils include fine sands, fine silty sands, saturated silts and peat. Buildings should not be constructed over or within 3m of drains or sewers in such soils unless special measures are taken in the design and construction of foundations to prevent undue risk to the building in the event of failure of the drain or sewer. Special measures will not be needed if the invert of the drain or sewer is:

a. above the level of the foundations; and

b. above the groundwater level; and

c. no more than 1m deep.

1.2 A building constructed over or within 3m of:

a. any rising main (except those used solely to drain the building);

b. any drain or sewer constructed from brick or masonry;

c. any drain or sewer in poor condition (e.g. the pipes are cracked, fractured, deformed more than 5% or misaligned)

would be exposed to a high level of risk in the event of failure of the drain or sewer. Buildings should not be constructed in such a position unless special measures are taken.

Maintaining access

1.3 Buildings or extensions should not be constructed over a manhole or inspection chamber or other access fitting on any sewer (serving more than one property). Approved Document H1 Section 2, paragraph 2.53 provides that access points to sewers (serving more than one property) should be in places where they are accessible and apparent for use in an emergency. Buildings and extensions should not be located where they would remove such a provision where this already exists, unless an alternative access point can be provided on the line of the sewer at a location acceptable to the owner (i.e. the sewerage undertaker in the case of a public sewer).

1.4 A satisfactory diversionary route should be available so that the drain or sewer could be reconstructed without affecting the building. This route should not pass within 3m from the building. Where the drain or sewer is more than 1.5m deep and the drain or sewer is accessible to mechanical excavators the alternative route should also have such access.

1.5 The length of drain or sewer under a building should not exceed 6m except with the permission of the owners of the drain or sewer (i.e. the sewerage undertaker in case of a public sewer).

1.6 Buildings or extensions should not be constructed over or within 3m of any drain or sewer more than 3m deep, or greater than 225mm in diameter except with the permission of the owners of the drain or sewer (i.e. the sewerage undertaker in the case of a public sewer).

Protection of the drain or sewer during construction

1.7 Any drain or sewer should be protected from damage by construction traffic and heavy machinery. Protection may be provided by providing barriers to keep such traffic away from the line of the sewer. Heavy materials should not be stored over drains or sewers.

1.8 Where piling works are being carried out care should be taken to avoid damage to any drain or sewer. The position of the drain or sewer should be established by survey. If the drain or sewer is within 1m of the piling, trial holes should be excavated to establish the exact position of the sewer. The location of any connections should also be established. Piling should not be carried out where the distance from the outside of the sewer to the outside of the pile is less than twice the diameter of the pile.

Protection from settlement

1.9 Where a drain or sewer runs under a building at least 100mm of granular or other suitable flexible filling should be provided round the pipe. On sites where excessive subsidence is possible additional flexible joints may be advisable or other solutions adopted such as suspended drainage. Where the crown of the pipe is within 300mm of the underside of the slab, special protection should be provided (see Approved Document H1, Section 2, paragraph 2.44).

1.10 Where a drain or sewer running below a building is less than 2m deep, the foundation should be extended locally so that the drain or sewer passes through the wall (see paragraph 1.11).

1.11 Where a drain or sewer runs through a wall or foundation suitable measures should be taken to prevent damage or misalignment. For further guidance see Approved Document H1 paragraph 2.24.

1.12 Where the drain or sewer is more than 2m deep to invert and passes beneath the foundations, the foundations should be designed as a lintel spanning over the line of the drain or sewer. The span of the lintel should extend at least 1.5m either side of the pipe and should be designed so that no load is transmitted onto the drain or sewer.

1.13 A drain trench should not be excavated lower than the foundations of any building nearby. For further guidance see Approved Document H1 paragraph 2.25.

The Requirement

This Approved Document, which took effect on 1 April 2002, deals with the following Requirement which is contained in the Building Regulations 2010.

Requirement	Limits on application
Separate systems of drainage	
H5. Any system for discharging water to a sewer which is provided pursuant to paragraph H3 shall be separate from that provided for the conveyance of foul water from the building.	Requirement H5 applies only to a system provided in connection with the erection or extension of a building where it is reasonably practicable for the system to discharge directly or indirectly to a sewer for the separate conveyance of surface water which is:
	(a) shown on a map of sewers; or
	(b) under construction either by the sewerage undertaker or by some other person (where the sewer is the subject of an agreement to make a declaration of vesting pursuant to Section 104 of the Water Industry Act 1991 (**b**)).

(**b**) Section 104 was amended by Section 96 of the Schedule 9 to the Water Act 2003. and is prospectively amended by Section 42 of the Flood and Water Management Act 2010 (c. 29).

Guidance

Performance

In the Secretary of State's view the requirements of H5 will be met if separate systems of drains and sewers are provided for foul water and rainwater where:

a. the rainwater is not contaminated; and

b. the drainage is to be connected either directly or indirectly to the public sewer system and either:

   i. the public sewer system in the area comprises separate systems for foul water and surface water; or

   ii. a system of sewers which provides for the separate conveyance of surface water is under construction either by the sewerage undertaker or by some other person (where the sewer is the subject of an agreement to make a declaration of vesting pursuant to Section 104 of the Water Industry Act 1991).

Introduction to provisions

0.1 These provisions are to help minimise the volume of rainwater entering the public foul sewer system as this can overload the capacity of the sewer and cause flooding.

Provision where separate sewer systems are provided

1.1 Where the buildings are to be drained to the public sewer system, and the sewerage undertaker has provided a separate system of sewers, separate drainage systems will be necessary in order to comply with the requirements of Section 106 (Right to communicate with public sewers) of the Water Industry Act 1991 (see appendix H1-C paragraph C.7).

Provision where separate sewer systems are proposed

1.2   Separate foul and rainwater drainage systems should also be provided where there is a combined sewer system at present but a system of sewers which provides for the separate conveyance of surface water is under construction either by the sewerage undertaker or by some other person (where the sewer is the subject of an agreement to make declaration of vesting pursuant to Section 104 of the Water Industry Act 1991).

1.3   These separate drainage systems will both initially connect to the existing combined sewer system. However, when the separate sewer systems are completed, the drainage will be reconnected to the new sewers, minimising the disruption to the occupiers.

Contaminated runoff

1.4   Approved Document H3 paragraph 3.21 deals with drainage from areas where materials are stored which could contaminate runoff. This could cause pollution if discharged to a surface water sewer. Where such flows are to be discharged into the foul sewer system, the consent of the sewerage undertaker should first be obtained in accordance with Section 106 (Right to communicate with public sewers) of the Water Industry Act 1991 (see appendix H1-C paragraph C.7). The sewerage undertaker should also be consulted where such flows are to be discharged into a foul drain which, though it would initially connect to a combined sewer, is intended would eventually be reconnected to a proposed foul sewer.

The Requirement

This Approved Document, which took effect on 1 April 2002, deals with the following Requirement which is contained in the Building Regulations 2010.

Requirement	Limits on application
Solid waste storage **H6.** (1) Adequate provision shall be made for storage of solid waste. (2) Adequate means of access shall be provided: (a) for people in the building to the place of storage; and (b) from the place of storage to a collection point (where one has been specified by the waste collection authority under Section 46 (household waste) or Section 47 (commercial waste) of the Environmental Protection Act 1990 (**a**) or to a street (where no collection point has been specified).	

(**a**) 1990 c. 43; section 46 was amended by Section 19 of the London Local Authorities Act 2007 (2007 c. ii) and Section 47 was amended by Section 21 of that Act. Section 46 was also amended by Section 76 and Schedule 5 to the Climate Change Act 2008 (c. 28).

Guidance

Performance

In the Secretary of State's view the requirements of H6 will be met if the solid waste storage is:

a. designed and sited so as not to be prejudicial to health or local amenity;

b. of sufficient area having regard to the requirements of the waste collection authority for the number and size of receptacles under Sections 46 and 47 of the Environmental Protection Act 1990;

c. sited so as to be accessible for use by people in the building and of ready access for removal to the collection point specified by the waste collection authority under Sections 46 and 47 of the Environmental Protection Act 1990.

Introduction to provisions

0.1 The efficacy of a refuse storage system is dependent on its capacity and the ease of removal in relation to the collection service provided by the waste collection authority.

0.2 The waste collection authority has powers under Section 46 (Receptacles for household waste) and Section 47 (Receptacles for commercial or industrial waste) to specify the type and number of receptacles to be used and the location where the waste should be placed for collection. **Consultation should take place with the waste collection authority to determine their requirements.**

0.3 H6 applies to the erection or extension of a building and to all material changes of use described in Regulation 5.

Domestic developments

Capacity

1.1 For domestic developments space should be provided for storage of containers for separated waste (i.e. waste which can be recycled is stored separately from waste which cannot) with a combined capacity of 0.25m³ per dwelling or such other capacity as may be agreed with the waste collection authority. Where collections are less frequent than once per week, this allowance should be increased accordingly.

1.2 Low rise domestic developments – In low rise domestic developments (houses, bungalows and flats up to 4th floor) any dwelling should have, or have access to, a location where at least two movable individual or communal waste containers, meeting the requirements of the waste collection authority, can be stored.

1.3 Where separate storage areas are provided for each dwelling, an area of 1.2m x 1.2m should be sufficient to provide for storage of waste containers and provide space for access.

1.4 Where communal storage areas are provided space requirements should be determined in consultation with the waste collection authority.

1.5 High rise domestic developments – in multi-storey domestic developments dwellings up to the 4th floor may each have their own waste container or may share a waste container.

1.6 Dwellings above the 4th storey may share a single waste container for non-recyclable waste fed by chute, with separate storage for any waste which can be recycled. Alternatively storage compounds or rooms should be provided. In such a case a satisfactory management arrangement for conveying refuse to the storage area should be assured.

1.7 The use of 'Residents Only' recycling centres (areas where residents may bring their recyclable waste for storage in large containers, e.g. bottle banks) in large blocks has been found to be effective in some areas.

Siting

1.8 Storage areas for waste containers and chutes should be sited so that the distance householders are required to carry refuse does not usually exceed 30m (excluding any vertical distance). Containers should be within 25m of the waste collection point specified by the waste collection authority.

1.9 The location for storage of waste containers should be sited so that, unless it is completely unavoidable, the containers can be taken to the collection point without being taken through a building, unless it is a porch or garage, or a car port or other open covered space (this provision applies only to new buildings except that extensions or conversions should not remove such a facility where one already exists).

1.10 For waste containers up to 250 litres, steps should be avoided between the container store and collection point wherever possible and should not exceed 3 in number. Slopes should not exceed 1:12. Exceptionally this may be exceeded provided that the lengths are not excessive and it is not part of a series of slopes. (See also Approved Document K1 Section 2.) For storage areas where larger containers are to be used steps should be avoided. Where this is not otherwise possible, the storage area should be relocated.

1.11 The collection point should be reasonably accessible to the size of waste collection vehicles typically used by the waste collection authority.

1.12 External storage areas for waste containers should be away from windows and ventilators and preferably be in shade or under shelter. Storage areas should not interfere with pedestrian or vehicle access to buildings.

Design

1.13 Unsightly bins can damage the visual amenity of an area and contribute to increased levels of anti-social nuisance such as odour and litter, so bin storage should be planned carefully. Where the location for storage is in a publicly accessible area or in an open area around a building (e.g. in a front garden) an enclosure or shelter should be considered. Best practice guidance is given in NHBC Foundation report NF60.

1.14 Where enclosures, compounds or storage rooms are provided they should allow room for filling and emptying and provide a clear space of 150mm between and around the containers. Enclosures, compounds or storage rooms for communal containers should be a minimum of 2m high. Enclosures for individual containers should be sufficiently high to allow the lid to be opened for filling. The enclosure should be permanently ventilated at the top and bottom and should have a paved impervious floor.

1.15 Communal storage areas should have provision for washing down and draining the floor into a system suitable for receiving a polluted effluent. Gullies should incorporate a trap which maintains a seal even during prolonged periods of disuse.

1.16 Any room for the open storage of waste should be secure to prevent access by vermin. Any compound for the storage of waste should be secure to prevent access by vermin unless the waste is to be stored in secure containers with close fitting lids.

1.17 Where storage rooms are provided, separate rooms should be provided for the storage of waste which cannot be recycled, and waste which can be recycled.

1.18 High-rise domestic developments – where chutes are provided they should be at least 450mm diameter and should have a smooth non-absorbent surface and close fitting access doors at each storey which has a dwelling and be ventilated at the top and bottom.

Non-domestic developments

1.19 In other types of development, and particularly where special problems such as high density developments influence the provision of a system, it is essential that the waste collection authority is consulted for guidance on resolving the following points.

a. The volume and nature of the waste and the storage capacity required, based on the frequency of collection and the size and type of waste container.

b. Any requirements for segregation of waste which can be recycled.

c. The method of waste storage, including any on-site treatment proposed, related to the intended layout and building density.

d. The location of waste storage areas, waste treatment areas and waste collection points and the access to these locations for operatives and vehicles.

e. Hygiene arrangements in the waste storage and waste treatment areas.

f. Fire hazards and protection measures.

1.20 Waste storage areas should have an impervious floor and should have provision for washing down and draining the floor into a system suitable for receiving a polluted effluent. Gullies should incorporate a trap which maintains a seal even during prolonged periods of disuse.

1.21 Any room for the open storage of waste should be secure to prevent access by vermin. Any compound for the storage of waste should be secure to prevent access by vermin unless the waste is to be stored in secure containers with close fitting lids.

1.22 Waste storage areas should be marked and signs should be provided.

Alternative approach

1.23 Recommendations and data on these items can be found in BS 5906:2005 *Code of practice for waste management in buildings*.

Appendix H6-A: Relevant waste collection legislation

Collection of household waste

A.1 Under Section 45 (Collection of controlled waste) of the Environmental Protection Act 1990, local authorities have a general duty to collect household waste within their area without charge.

A.2 Under Section 46 (Receptacles for household waste) of the Environmental Protection Act 1990, the local authority may require:

a. waste of certain types to be stored separately so that it can be recycled;

b. occupiers of dwellings to provide containers of a specified type for storage of waste;

c. additional containers to be provided for separate storage of recyclable waste;

d. locations where containers should be placed for emptying.

Collection of commercial and industrial waste

A.3 Under Section 45 (Collection of controlled waste) of the Environmental Protection Act 1990, local authorities may also have a duty to collect commercial waste within their area where requested and they may also collect industrial waste. A charge may be levied for such services.

A.4 Under Section 47 (Receptacles for commercial or industrial waste) of the Environmental Protection Act 1990, the local authority may still require:

a. waste of certain types to be stored separately so that it can be recycled;

b. occupiers to provide containers of a specified type for storage of waste;

c. additional containers to be provided for separate storage of recyclable waste;

d. locations where containers should be placed for emptying.

Access for removal of waste to be maintained

A.5 Under Section 23 (Provision of facilities for refuse) subsection (3) of the Building Act 1984, it is unlawful to obstruct the access (such as those specified in Requirement H6 of the Building Regulations) provided for removal of waste without the consent of the local authority. In giving their consent, the local authority may specify conditions regarding the provision of an alternative means of access for removal of refuse.

Standards referred to

H1

BS 65:1991
Specification for vitrified clay pipes, fittings and ducts, also flexible mechanical joints for use solely with surface water pipes and fittings. AMD 8622 1995.

BS EN 274:1993
Sanitary tapware. Waste fittings for basins, bidets and baths. General technical specifications. (Withdrawn and superseded by BS EN 274-1:2002 Waste fittings for sanitary appliances. Requirements. AMD 14959 2004. BS EN 274-2:2002 Waste fitting for sanitary appliances. Test methods. AMD 14957 2004. BS EN 274-3:2002 Waste fittings for sanitary appliances. Quality control. AMD 14958 2004.)

BS EN 295-1:1991
Vitrified clay pipes and fittings and pipe joints for drains and sewers. Test requirements. AMD 9290 1996, AMD 9429 1995, AMD 10621 1999.

BS EN 295-2:1991
Vitrified clay pipes and fittings and pipe joints for drains and sewers. Quality control and sampling. AMD 10620 1999.

BS EN 295-3:1991
Vitrified clay pipes and fittings and pipe joints for drains and sewers. Test methods. AMD 10357 1999.

BS EN 295-6:1996
Vitrified clay pipes and fittings and pipe joints for drains and sewers. Requirements for vitrified clay manholes. AMD 15279 2004.

BS 416-1:1990
Discharge and ventilating pipes and fittings, sand-cast or spun in cast iron. Specification for spigot and socket systems.

BS 437:1978
Specification for cast iron spigot and socket drain pipes and fittings. AMD 5877 1988.

BS EN 598:1995
Ductile iron pipes, fittings, accessories and their joints for sewerage applications. Requirements and test methods.

BS EN 752-1:1996
Drain and sewer systems outside buildings. Generalities and definitions.

BS EN 752-2:1997
Drain and sewer systems outside buildings. Performance requirements.

BS EN 752-3:1997
Drain and sewer systems outside buildings. Planning. AMD 10984 2000, AMD 13038 2001.

BS EN 752-4:1998
Drain and sewer systems outside buildings. Hydraulic design and environmental considerations. AMD 15442 2005.

BS EN 752-5:1998
Drain and sewer systems outside buildings. Rehabilitation.

BS EN 752-6:1998
Drain and sewer systems outside buildings. Pumping installations.

BS EN 752-7:1998
Drain and sewer systems outside buildings. Maintenance and operations. AMD 10440 1999.

BS EN 877:1999
Cast iron pipes and fittings, their joints and accessories for the evacuation of water from buildings. Requirements, test methods and quality assurance.

BS 882:1992
Specification for aggregates from natural sources for concrete. AMD 13579 2002.
(Withdrawn and superseded by BS EN 1260:2002 Aggregates for concrete. AMD 15333 2004.)

BS EN 1057:1996
Copper and copper alloys. Seamless, round copper tubes for water and gas in sanitary and heating applications.

BS EN 1091:1997
Vacuum sewerage systems outside buildings.

BS EN 1254-1:1998
Copper and copper alloys. Plumbing fittings. Fittings with ends for capillary soldering or capillary brazing to copper tubes. AMD 10099 1998.

BS EN 1254-2:1998
Copper and copper alloys. Plumbing fittings. Fittings with compression ends for use with copper tubes.

BS EN 1254-3:1998
Copper and copper alloys. Plumbing fittings. Fittings with compression ends for use with plastics pipes.

BS EN 1254-4:1998
Copper and copper alloys. Plumbing fittings. Fittings combining other end connections with capillary or compression ends. AMD 10750 1999.

BS EN 1254-5:1998
Copper and copper alloys. Plumbing fittings. Fittings with short ends for capillary brazing to copper tubes. AMD 10100 1998.

BS EN 1295-1:1998
Structural design of buried pipelines under various conditions of loading. General requirements.

BS EN 1329-1:2000
Plastics piping systems for soil and waste discharge (low and high temperature) within the building structure. Unplasticized polyvinyl chloride (PVC-U). Specifications for pipes, fittings and the system.

BS EN 1401-1:1998
Plastics piping systems for non-pressure underground drainage and sewerage. Unplasticized poly(vinylchloride) (PVC-U). Specifications for pipes, fittings and the system. AMD 13794 2002.

BS EN 1451-1:2000
Plastics piping systems for soil and waste discharge (low and high temperature) within the building structure. Polypropylene (PP). Specifications for pipes, fittings and the system. AMD 13819 2002.

BS EN 1455-1:2000
Plastics piping systems for soil and waste (low and high temperature) within the building structure. Acrylonitrile-butadienestyrene (ABS). Specifications for pipes, fittings and the system. AMD 13818 2002.

BS EN 1519-1:2000
Plastics piping systems for soil and waste discharge (low and high temperature) within the building structure. Polyethylene (PE). Specifications for pipes, fittings and the system. AMD 13817 2002.

BS EN 1565-1:2000
Plastics piping systems for soil and waste discharge (low and high temperature) within the building structure. Styrene copolymer blends (SAN + PVC). Specifications for pipes, fittings and the system. AMD 13816 2002.

BS EN 1566-1:2000
Plastics piping systems for soil and waste discharge (low and high temperature) within the building structure. Chlorinated poly (vinyl chloride) (PVC-C). specification for pipes, fittings and the system. AMD 13815 2002.

BS EN 1610:1998
Construction and testing of drains and sewers.

BS EN 1671:1997
Pressure sewerage systems outside buildings.

BS EN 1825-1:2004
Installations for separation of grease. Principles of design, performance and testing, marking and quality control.

BS EN 1825-2:2002
Installations for separation of grease. Selection of nominal size, installation and maintenance.

BS EN 1852-1:1998
Plastics piping systems for non-pressure underground drainage and sewerage. Polypropylene (PP). Specifications for pipes, fittings and the system. AMD 14514 2003.

BS 3868:1995
Specification for prefabricated drainage stack units in galvanized steel.

BS 3921:1985
Specification for clay bricks.
(Current but partially superseded by BS EN 772-3:1998 Method of test for masonry units. Determination of net volume and percentage of voids of clay masonry units by hydrostatic weighing. BS EN 772-7:1998 Method of test for masonry units. Determination of water absorption of clay masonry damp proof course units by boiling in water.)

BS 5255:1989
Specification for thermo-plastics waste pipe and fittings.
(Current but partially superseded by BS EN 1329-1:2000 Plastics piping systems for soil and waste discharge (low and high temperature) within the building structure. Unplasticized poly(vinyl chloride) (PVC-U). Specifications for pipes, fittings and the system. BS EN 1455-1:2000 Plastics piping systems for soil and waste (low and high temperature) within the building structure. Acrylonitrile-butadiene-styrene (ABS). Specifications for pipes, fittings and the system. AMD 13818 2002. BS EN 1519-1:2000 Plastics piping systems for soil and waste discharge (low and high temperature) within the building structure. Polyethylene (PE). Specifications for pipes, fittings and the system. AMD 13817 2002. BS EN 1565-1:2000 Plastics piping systems for soil and waste discharge (low and high temperature) within the building structure. Styrene copolymer blends (SAN + PVC). Specifications for pipes, fittings and the system. AMD 13816 2002. BS EN 1566-1:2000 Plastics piping systems for soil and waste discharge (low and high temperature) within the building structure. Chlorinated poly(vinyl chloride) (PVC-C). Specification for pipes, fittings and the system. AMD 13815 2002.)

BS 5911-2:1982
Precast concrete pipes, fittings and ancillary products. Specification for inspection chambers. AMD 5146 1986, AMD 8077 1994, AMD 11030 2001.
(Withdrawn and superseded by BS 5911-4:2002 Concrete pipes and ancillary concrete products. Specification for unreinforced and reinforced concrete inspection chambers. AMD 15038 2004. BS EN 1917:2002 Concrete manholes and inspection chambers, unreinforced, steel fibre and reinforced. AMD 15289 2004.)

BS 5911-100:1988
Precast concrete pipes, fittings and ancillary products. Specification for unreinforced and reinforced pipes and fittings with flexible joints. AMD 6269 1989, AMD 7588 1993.
(Withdrawn and superseded by BS 5911-1:2002 Concrete pipes and ancillary concrete products. Specification for unreinforced and reinforced concrete pipes (including jacking pipes) and fittings with flexible joints. AMD 15040 2004. BS EN 1916:2002 Concrete pipes and fittings, unreinforced, steel fibre and reinforced. AMD 15288 2004.)

BS 5911-120:1989
Precast concrete pipes, fittings and ancillary products. Specification for reinforced jacking pipes with flexible joints. AMD 9020 1996. (Withdrawn and superseded by BS 5911-1:2002 Concrete pipes and ancillary concrete products. Specification for unreinforced and reinforced concrete pipes (including jacking pipes) and fittings with flexible joints. AMD 15040 2004. BS EN 1916:2002 Concrete pipes and fittings, unreinforced, steel fibre and reinforced. AMD 15288 2004.)

BS 5911-200:1994
Precast concrete pipes, fittings and ancillary products. Specification for unreinforced and reinforced manholes and soakaways of circular cross section. AMD 11031 2001, AMD 13205 2001. (Withdrawn and superseded by BS 5911-3:2002 Concrete pipes and ancillary concrete products. Specification for unreinforced and reinforced concrete manholes and soakaways. AMD 15039 2004. BS EN 1917:2002 Concrete manholes and inspection chambers, unreinforced, steel fibre and reinforced. AMD 15289 2004.)

BS 6798:2000
Specification for installation of gas-fired hot water boilers of rated input not exceeding 70kW. AMD 14908 2005.

BS 7158:2001
Plastics inspection chambers for drains and sewers. Specification. (Current but superseded by BS EN 13598-1:2003 Plastics piping systems for non-pressure underground drainage and sewerage. Unplasticized poly(vinyl chloride) (PVC-U), polypropylene (PP) and polyethylene (PE). Specifications for ancillary fittings including shallow inspection chambers.)

BS 8000-13:1989
Workmanship on building sites. Code of practice for above ground drainage and sanitary appliances.

BS 8000-14:1989
Workmanship on building sites. Code of practice for below ground drainage.

BS 8110-1:1997
Structural use of concrete. Code of practice for design and construction. AMD 9882 1998, AMD 13468 2002, AMD 16016 2005.

BS EN 12050-1:2001
Wastewater lifting plants for buildings and sites. Principles of construction and testing. Lifting plants for wastewater containing faecal matter.

BS EN 12050-2:2001
Wastewater lifting plants for buildings and sites. Principles of construction and testing. Lifting plants for faecal-free wastewater.

BS EN 12050-3:2001
Wastewater lifting plants for buildings and sites. Principles of construction and testing. Lifting plants for wastewater containing faecal matter for limited applications.

BS EN 12056-1:2000
Gravity drainage systems inside buildings. General and performance requirements.

BS EN 12056-2:2000
Gravity drainage systems inside buildings. Sanitary pipework, layout and calculation.

BS EN 12056-3:2000
Gravity drainage systems inside buildings. Roof drainage, layout and calculation.

BS EN 12056-4:2000
Gravity drainage systems inside buildings. Wastewater lifting plants. Layout and calculation.

BS EN 12056-5:2000
Gravity drainage systems inside buildings. Installation and testing, instructions for operation, maintenance and use.

BS EN 12109:1999
Vacuum drainage systems inside buildings.

BS EN 12380:2002
Air admittance valves for drainage systems. Requirements, test methods and valuation of conformity.

BS EN 13564-1:2002
Anti-flooding devices for buildings. Quality assurance.

BS EN 13564-2:2002
Anti-flooding devices for buildings. Test methods.

BS EN 13564-3:2002
Anti-flooding devices for buildings. Quality assurance.

H2

BS 5328-1:1997
Concrete. Guide to specifying concrete. AMD 10364 1999, AMD 13876, AMD 14163 2002. (Withdrawn and superseded by BS 8500-1:2002 Concrete. Complementary British Standard to BS EN 206-1. Method of specifying and guidance for the specifier. AMD 14639 2003. BS 8500-2:2002 Concrete. Complementary British Standard to BS EN 206-1. Specification for constituent materials and concrete. AMD 14640 2003. BS EN 206-1:2000 Concrete. Specification, performance, production and conformity. AMD 13189 2001, AMD 14857 2004, AMD 15359 2004, AMD 15406 2004.)

BS 5328-2:1997
Concrete. Methods for specifying concrete mixes. AMD 9691 1997, AMD 10365 1999, AMD 10612 1999, AMD 13877. (Withdrawn and superseded by BS 8500-1:2002 Concrete. Complementary British Standard to BS EN 206-1. Method of specifying and guidance for the specifier. AMD 14639 2003. BS 8500-2:2002 Concrete. Complementary British Standard to BS EN 206-1. Specification for constituent materials and concrete. AMD 14640 2003. BS EN 206-1:2000 Concrete. Specification, performance, production and conformity. AMD 13189 2001, AMD 14857 2004, AMD 15359 2004, AMD 15406 2004.)

BS 5328-3:1990
Concrete. Specification for the procedures to be used in producing and transporting concrete. AMD 6927 1991, AMD 7176 1992, AMD 9312, AMD 10366 1999, AMD 10708 1999, AMD 13878 2002. (Withdrawn and superseded by BS 8500-1:2002 Concrete. Complementary British Standard to BS EN 206-1. Method of specifying and guidance for the specifier. AMD 14639 2003. BS 8500-2:2002 Concrete. Complementary British Standard to BS EN 206-1. Specification for constituent materials and concrete. AMD 14640 2003. BS EN 206-1:2000 Concrete. Specification, performance, production and conformity. AMD 13189 2001, AMD 14857 2004, AMD 15359 2004, AMD 15406 2004.)

BS 5328-4:1990
Concrete. Specification for the procedures to be used in sampling, testing and assessing compliance of concrete. AMD 6928 1991, AMD 8760 1995, AMD 9313, AMD 10367 1999, AMD 10611 1999. (Withdrawn and superseded by BS 8500-1:2002 Concrete. Complementary British Standard to BS EN 206-1. Method of specifying and guidance for the specifier. AMD 14639 2003. BS 8500-2:2002 Concrete. Complementary British Standard to BS EN 206-1. Specification for constituent materials and concrete. AMD 14640 2003. BS EN 206-1:2000 Concrete. Specification, performance, production and conformity. AMD 13189 2001, AMD 14857 2004, AMD 15359 2004, AMD 15406 2004.)

BS 6297:1983
Code of practice for design and installation of small sewage treatment works and cesspools. AMD 1650 1990.

BS 7781:1994
Procedure for type testing of small biological domestic wastewater treatment plants.

BS EN 12566-1:2000
Small wastewater treatment plants less than 50 PE. Part Prefabricated septic tanks. AMD 14918 2004.

H3

BS EN 752-1:1996
Drain and sewer systems outside buildings. Generalities and definitions.

BS EN 752-2:1997
Drain and sewer systems outside buildings. Performance requirements.

BS EN 752-3:1997
Drain and sewer systems outside buildings. Planning. AMD 10984 2000, AMD 13038 2001.

BS EN 752-4:1998
Drain and sewer systems outside buildings. Hydraulic design and environmental considerations. AMD 15442 2005.

BS EN 752-5:1998
Drain and sewer systems outside buildings. Rehabilitation.

BS EN 752-6:1998
Drain and sewer systems outside buildings. Pumping installations.

BS EN 752-7:1998
Drain and sewer systems outside buildings. Maintenance and operations. AMD 10440 1999.

BS EN 858:2001
Separator systems for light liquids (e.g. oil and petrol). Principles of product design, performance and testing, making and quality control. AMD 15525 2005.

BS EN 858-2:2003
Separator systems for light liquids (e.g. oil and petrol). Selection of nominal size, installation, operation and maintenance.

BS EN 1295-1:1998
Structural design of buried pipelines under various conditions of loading. General requirements.

BS EN 1610:1998
Construction and testing of drains and sewers.

BS EN 12056-1:2000
Gravity drainage systems inside buildings. General and performance requirements.

BS EN 12056-2:2000
Gravity drainage systems inside buildings. Sanitary pipework, layout and calculation.

BS EN 12056-3:2000
Gravity drainage systems inside buildings. Roof drainage, layout and calculation.

BS EN 12056-4:2000
Gravity drainage systems inside buildings. Wastewater lifting plants. Layout and calculation.

BS EN 12056-5:2000
Gravity drainage systems inside buildings. Installation and testing, instructions for operation, maintenance and use.

H4

–

H5

–

H6

BS 5906:2005
Code of practice for waste management in buildings.

Other publications referred to

H1

Water Regulations Advisory Scheme (WRAS)

Information and Guidance Note 09-02-05 *Marking and identification of pipe work for reclaimed and (grey water) systems*, 1999.

Information and Guidance Note 09-02-04 *Reclaimed water systems. Information about installing, modifying or maintaining reclaimed water systems*, 1999.

WRAS documents available from WRAS, Fern Close, Pen-y-Fan Industrial Estate, Oakdale, Gwent, NP11 3EH, Tel 01495 248454, Fax 01495 249235, email info@wras.co.uk. Available to download from www.wras.co.uk/

Water Research Council (WRc)

Sewers for adoption. A design and construction guide for developers, 5th edition, 2001. ISBN 1 89892 043 5

H2

BRE

Good Building Guide GBG 42 Part 1 *Reed beds: application and specification*, 2000. ISBN 1 86081 436 0

Good Building Guide GBG 42 Part 1 *Reed beds: design, construction*, 2000. ISBN 1 86081 437 9

Environment Agency

Pollution Prevention Guidelines PPG 4 *Disposal of sewage where no mains drainage is available*, 2001. Available to download from www.netregs.gov.uk

H3

BRE

Digest 365 *Soakaway design*, 1991 (minor revisions 2003). ISBN 1 86081 604 5

CIRIA

Publication C522 *Sustainable urban drainage systems – design manual for England and Wales*, 2000. ISBN 0 86017 522 7

Report 156 *Infiltration drainage – Manual of good practice*, 1996. ISBN 0 86017 457 3

Environment Agency

Pollution Prevention Guidelines PPG 3 *Use and design of oil separators in surface water drainage systems*, 2000. Available to download from www.netregs.gov.uk

H R Wallingford

Report SR 463 *Performance of syphonic drainage systems for roof gutters*.

Department for Communities and Local Government

Planning Policy Guidance 14, Development on unstable land – Annex 1: *Landslides and planning*, 1996. ISBN 0 11753 259 2. Available to download from www.gov.uk

Water Regulations Advisory Scheme (WRAS)

Information and Guidance Note 09-02-05 *Marking and identification of pipe work for reclaimed and (greywater) systems*, 1999.

Information and Guidance Note 09-02-04 *Reclaimed water systems. Information about installing, modifying or maintaining reclaimed water systems*, 1999.

H4

–

H5

–

H6

NHBC Foundation

Report NF60 *Avoiding rubbish design. Providing for bin storage on new housing developments,* 2015. Available to download from www.nhbcfoundation.org